The Habanero Cookbook

BOOKS BY
DAVE DEWITT & NANCY GERLACH:

The Fiery Cuisines
Fiery Appetizers
The Whole Chile Pepper Book
Just North of the Border

THE
HABANERO
COOKBOOK

Dave DeWitt
and
Nancy Gerlach

TEN SPEED PRESS
Berkeley, CA

Portions of this book first appeared in *Chile Pepper* magazine and are used here with permission.

TEN SPEED PRESS
P.O. Box 7123
Berkeley, CA 94707

Text and cover design by Nancy Austin
Production by Catherine Jacobes
Photo credits:
Page i: Rica Red habaneros, by Dave DeWitt; page vi: *fatalii* pepper, by Dave DeWitt; page 1: pod types of *Capsicum chinense,* the Chile Institute, 1993; page 2: Chris Way's datil Harley, by Dave DeWitt; page 37: habaneros at the Yucatecan market, by Jeffrey Gerlach; page 38: unnamed South American *chinense* from New Mexico State University, by Dave DeWitt; page 132: Peruvian red *chinense* by Dave DeWitt.
Photographs on pages 12, 23, 31, 34, 40, 44, 54, 58, 69, 73, 76, 77, 78, 84, 86, 88, 95, 101, 115, 129, 130, 132, 136, 143, and 148 by Dave DeWitt
Photograph on page 4 by Jeffrey Gerlach
Photograph on page 51 by Chel Beeson
Illustrations on page 61 © 1994 by Ellen Joy Sasaki

Library of Congress Cataloging-in-Publication Data

    DeWitt, Dave.
        The habanero cookbook / by Dave DeWitt and Nancy Gerlach.
            p.   cm.
        Includes bibliographical references and index.
        ISBN 0-89815-638-6
        1. Cookery (Hot peppers) 2. Hot peppers I. Gerlach, Nancy.
    II. Title.
    TX803.P46D48   1994
    641.6'384--dc20   94-13961
                                                                              CIP

FIRST PRINTING 1995

Printed in Hong Kong by South China Printing Company
1 2 3 4 5 6 — 99 98 97 96 95

To all lovers of the hottest chile peppers in the world

CONTENTS

ACKNOWLEDGMENTS

Thanks to the following habanero lovers who helped with this book:

Jim Ault, Peggy Barnes, Chel Beeson, Michael Bordes, Paul Bosland, Thomas Brown, Jeff Campbell, Jack Curry, Rudolfo DeGaray, Chuck Evans, Frank Garcia Jr., Jeff Gerlach, Graham H. Jacks, Stuart Jeffrey, Cody Jordan, Bob Kennedy, Paul Klinger Jr., Joe Litwin, Arlene Lutz, Vernon and Irene Montrichard, Jorge Morera, Johnny Nahous, Marie Permenter, Jackie Pestka, Bess Petlak, Steve Phillips, Brian Polcyn, Joe Roach, Glenn P. Rhodes, Richard Rice, Chris Schlesinger, Marie and Gerry Sharp, Jay Solomon, Robert Spiegel, Arnold L. Talbott, Paul and Melba Vigneault, Chris Way, Mary Jane Wilan, and F. P. Williamson.

INTRODUCTION

Welcome to a book devoted solely to a single chile pepper! The fact that this work even exists is a tribute to loyal chileheads who continue spread the word about the joys of hot and spicy food and who promote the burgeoning interest in peppers. At this writing, in addition to posters, postcards, and calendars devoted to peppers, there are at least ten books on the subject in print, including a field guide, a scholarly botanical study, a gardening guide, several chile histories, a full-color coffee table book, and several cookbooks. Never before, however, has a whole book been devoted to just one pepper—but what a pepper!

In less than a decade, the habanero has emerged from relative obscurity to become one of the most popular and renowned chiles in the United States. At fraternity parties at Ohio University, the students' masculinity is not tested by chugging beer, but by habanero-eating contests. At the Prince of Wales Pub in San Mateo, California, where bangers-and-mash and other British food prevails, the specialty of the house is a decidedly non-British delicacy: the habanero hamburger. Customers who can finish the hottest hamburger are awarded a bumper sticker that reads: I SURVIVED THE HABANERO HAMBURGER. Such is the level of habanero madness in this country.

Fresh habaneros are now common in supermarkets in many parts of the United States and Canada, and the whole pods are also available dried and pickled. Imports of habanero relatives such as Scotch bonnets and Congo peppers are escalating and products containing habaneros—especially hot sauces—are popping up everywhere. What is driving this mania? Why the fanatic interest in habaneros?

First and foremost, habaneros are renowned because they are by far the world's hottest pepper. "People always do want it hotter; that's the reason habaneros caught on," observes Jeff Campbell, a habanero grower and food manufacturer in the Texas Hill Country. The heat of habaneros can be adjusted, of course, by dilution with other ingredients, but the very fact that they are the world's hottest peppers is the key to their mystique. "In the amusement park of the chile peppers, this is the roller coaster, Ferris wheel, and the teacup ride all wrapped up into one," says Jay Solomon, author of *A Taste of the Tropics.*

Additionally, though, habaneros have a unique aroma and taste. "In spite of their fierce, intense heat, they have a wonderful, distinctive flavor with tropical fruit overtones," notes Mark Miller, chef and owner of the Coyote Cafe in Santa Fe. Their wonderful fruity flavor (in addition to their heat) is the reason they are used in the exotic and delicious cuisines of the Caribbean, Mexico, Latin America, and even parts of the United States. We have chosen the best from each to give you a good sampling of the habanero's versatility—as it joins with meats, fish, vegetables, fruits, and other foods.

In the past, cookbook authors have been forced to recommend unacceptable substitutes such as jalapeños for habaneros. But now that fresh habaneros are more readily available in this country (see Appendix), we have written *The Habanero Cookbook* so that American cooks will finally be able to experience the true taste of habanero recipes. (We have taken care, however, to adjust the amount of the peppers in each recipe so that we don't burn everyone out completely!)

We welcome you to the hot and delicious world of habaneros. For those of you already familiar with the hottest pepper, we offer a multitude of tantalizing ways to enjoy their mouthwatering heat. For those of you new to habaneros, prepare to be converted.

Habaneros Unleashed:

A History and Description

of the Hottest Peppers

on Earth

A Habanero by Any Other Name...

Welcome to a world of bright colors, fruity flavors, and intense heat. Welcome to the world of habaneros...or can we use that word? Habaneros and their kin are all *types* of peppers within *Capsicum chinense*, which is one of the five *species* of peppers that has been domesticated. As is true with all peppers, the names of those in the *chinense* species are extremely confusing. Note that, because there is no manual or field guide that matches the local names of peppers with photographs, we had to depend for the most part on amateur horticulturists and seed savers for the identification of the *chinense* varieties pictured in this book.

The *chinense* species was first noted in 1768 in *A Gardener's Dictionary*, by Phillip Miller, who identified it as *Capsicum angulofum*, a West Indian pepper with wrinkled leaves and a bonnetlike shape. The species was then misnamed *Capsicum chinense* in 1776 by Nikolaus von Jacquin, a Dutch physician who collected plants in the Caribbean for Emperor Francis I from 1754 to 1759. Jacquin, who first described the species as "chinense" in his work, *Hortus botanicus vindobonensis*, wrote, inexplicably, "I have taken the plant's name from its homeland."

Why would Jacquin write that a plant native to the West Indies was from China? Jacquin had never collected plants in China, and because the first Chinese laborers to arrive in the West Indies would not reach Cuba until the early 1800s, it is unlikely that he crossed paths with any suspected Chinese "importers" of the *chinense* species. To further confuse the issue, some botanists spell the species name "sinense." Because it is unlikely that this pepper mystery will ever be solved, we are stuck with a totally inaccurate species name for an alleged Chinese pepper that simply isn't from China. To date, no taxonomist has gone out on a limb to correct this obvious error.

So it's up to us. We propose changing the botanical name of the

Vegetable market in Merida, Yucatán, Mexico.

species to *Capsicum cheiro*. *Cheiro* is a Portuguese word meaning "odor" or "aroma," and in regards to peppers the word is used in Brazil to refer to pods of the *chinense* species with their characteristic fruity aroma. Since the *chinense* varieties share this odiferous trait, changing the species name to *cheiro* would make sense.

The word habanero (sometimes erroneously spelled habañero), is commonly used in English for the entire *chinense* species. That appellation is technically a misnomer, because there are dozens—if not hundreds—of pod types within the species, and the name "habanero" really refers to one specific pod type from the Yucatán Peninsula. The Scotch bonnet, for example, is another pod type in the same species. Because consumers in the United States are most familiar with the habanero type, however, "habanero" has become the common term for the entire *chinense* species, and that is why we use it in that manner in the title of this book.

Worldwide, there is a plethora of common names for *chinense* varieties. Local names in Spanish, Portuguese, and Indian dialects translate to such things as "fish eye," "parakeet's eye," and "blowgun pepper." Below are the common names for the *chinense* varieties found in various locales:

NAME	LOCATION
ají chombo	Panama
ají yaquitania	Brazil
bonda man Jacques	Martinique, Guadeloupe
booney or bonney pepper	Barbados
caballero	Guatemala
cachucha (or *ají cachucha*)	Cuba
charapilla	Peru
chile blanco	Caribbean
chinchi-uchu	Peru
Congo pepper	Trinidad, Fiji
le derrière de Madame Jacques	Guadeloupe
Dominica pepper	U.S. Virgin Islands
fatalii	Africa
goat pepper, billy goat pepper	Bahamas, Africa
Guinea pepper	Caribbean
habanero	Mexico, Belize, United States
murici	Brazil
panameño	Costa Rica
panco	Peru
piment bouc	Haiti
pimenta-de-bode	Brazil
pimenta do cheiro	Brazil
rocotillo	Peru, Caribbean
Scotch bonnet	Jamaica and Caribbean
tiger tooth	Guyana

Many of the common names have obscure origins—take goat peppers, for example. When *Chile Pepper* staff photographer Chel Beeson visited the Bahamas, he asked the locals about the name. "I got a bunch of funny answers," he told us when he returned, "like 'goats eat them' or 'they look like goat's heads.' I don't think the Bahamians know why they call them that. I bought some at the market and cut them up to put them in a sauce and my fingers burned for three days. I'd sit by the pool drinking a Goombay Smash with my fingers in the pool." The Haitian term for habanero, *piment bouc*, also translates as "billy goat pepper."

But what about the Cuban connection? Isn't that the origin of the word *habanero*, which means, literally, "from Havana"? Pepper experts have long debated the possible Cuban origin for the habaneros that are grown today in the Yucatán peninsula of Mexico and Belize. Pepper expert Jean Andrews observes that Cuba and Yucatán had close commercial ties in the 1800s (the channel separating them is only 150 miles wide). Mexican horticulturists Cancino Laborde and P. Pozo Compodonico state that the habanero is the only pepper in Yucatán without a Mayan name, which would indicate that it was imported. An early naturalist, Francisco Ximnez, wrote in his natural history of Guatemala in 1722 that he had heard of a pepper from Havana that was so strong that a single pod would "make a bull unable to eat." Some people theorize that the unnamed pod was the legendary early habanero. But some writers flatly doubt the connection and claim that habaneros have a Mexican origin and never were grown in Cuba. For example, Amal Naj claims in his book *Peppers,* that the habanero pepper "doesn't exist in Cuba."

Because of a decades-long prohibition against travel to Cuba, it's been difficult for American citizens to verify the existence of the *chinense* clan there. But we've always suspected that the *chinense* species must have *some* presence on an island only a hundred miles from Jamaica. In 1990, a *Chile Pepper* magazine reader sent us seeds that had been smuggled out of Cuba by refugees and passed on to him. We grew them, and they resembled red habaneros from Belize in color, shape, and heat. As further evidence of a Cuban connection, Javier Muñiz, co-owner of The Blazing Chile Brothers, a retail mail-order firm (see Appendix), is of Cuban descent and told us that a hot *chinense* variety in his homeland is called *ají cachucha,* translating as "cap chile," which neatly equates to the "Scotch bonnet" designation found in nearby Jamaica and much of the West Indies. The accumulation of evidence suggests that habaneros—or at least some *chinense* varieties—do indeed still grow in Cuba.

How Hot Are They?

The heat level of the *chinense* species has been the subject of much speculation and discussion. Phrases like "hottest pepper in the world" and "a thousand times hotter a jalapeño" have been bandied about for years, but they don't really tell the story. One sunny day in 1992, Dave was in the greenhouse of Dr. Paul Bosland, professor of horticulture at New Mexico State University, when the chile breeder picked what looked to be a ripe habanero off a plant and popped it into his mouth. Dave was astonished, knowing that Paul prefers his peppers fairly mild. After he had chewed and swallowed the pepper, Paul announced: "A nonpungent *chinense*." Dave followed suit and noted that the characteristic fruity aroma of the usually hot *chinense* species was still present in the mild pod.

Although the species is renowned for the high heat level of its pods, we should remember that all heat levels are found in the *chinense*, from zero to the hottest ever measured. The typical commercial habanero averages between 80,000 and 150,000 Scoville Units, as measured by high performance liquid chromatography, but what is the hottest *chinense* ever tested? In a series of experiments at New Mexico State University in 1992, Paul Bosland and Peggy Collins tested the same variety of *chinense*, an orange habanero from Yucatán, grown under different conditions. Grown outdoors in a field, the pods measured 357,992 Scoville Units. Grown in the greenhouse, they measured 260,825 Scoville Units. The variability of pungency approached 30 percent, which illustrates the environment's role in the heat levels of chile peppers. The next stage in their experiment will be to plant clones—genetically identical plants—and subject them to varying environmental factors. The hottest commercial *chinense* variety that we've ever heard about is the Red Savina habanero developed by GNS Spices (see pages 33–36), a pod of which measured 577,000 Scoville Units in 1994.

American chefs and cookbook authors love to wax poetic about the unique flavor of the fresh *chinense* varieties. Chef Mark Miller describes fresh habaneros as having "tropical fruit tones that mix well with food containing tropical fruits or tomatoes," and Scotch bonnets as possessing a "fruity and smoky flavor." Cookbook author Steven Raichlen agrees, describing the Scotch bonnets as "floral, aromatic, and almost smoky." As far as dried habaneros are concerned, Miller detects "tropical fruit flavors of coconut and papaya, a hint of berry, and an intense, fiery acidic heat."

How Much Hotter Than a Jalapeño Is the Habanero?

That's a tricky question, considering the fact that the heat levels of both vary so much. However, if we estimate that the average heat of a jalapeño is 3,000 Scoville Units and that of a habanero is 100,000 Scoville Units, simple division tells us that the habanero is thirty-three times hotter than a jalapeño. The mouth and lips might give a different rating!

Growing the Heat

The Plant

Because of the great diversity of the species, there is no typical *chinense* plant. The varieties range between one and four and a half feet tall, depending on environmental factors. Some perennial varieties have grown as tall as eight feet in tropical climates, but the average height in the U.S. garden is about two feet. It has multiple stems and grows upright. The leaves are pale to medium green, usually oval in shape, and are often large, reaching up to six inches long and four inches wide. They are usually crinkled, which is a distinguishing trait.

The flowers have white, slightly greenish corollas and purple anthers. The plant sets two to six fruits per node and this trait distinguishes it from the other *Capsicum* species, which usually only set one fruit per node. Chinense crosses prolifically with *annuum*, sporadically with *frutescens* and *baccatum*, and does not cross with *pubescens*.

The pods vary enormously in size and shape, ranging from chiltepin-sized berries one-quarter inch in diameter to wrinkled and elongated pods up to five inches long. The familiar habaneros are pendant, lantern-shaped or campanulate (a flattened bell shape), and some are pointed at the end. Caribbean *chinenses* are often flattened at the end and resemble a tam, or bonnet. Often the blossom ends of these pods are inverted. The pods are green at immaturity and mature to red, orange, yellow, or white. *Chinense* pods are characterized by a distinctive, fruity aroma that is often described as apricotlike.

The Home Garden

Although the Mexican habanero varieties Uxmal and INIA have been developed, neither is commercially available to home gardeners in the

United States. In the U.S., most commercial habanero seeds are generic (meaning that their precise origin is not specified), although some varieties such as Red Savina are appearing in seed catalogs. For growers who wish to find exotic *chinense* seeds, we suggest Seed Saver's Exchange or the U.S. Department of Agriculture's Plant Introduction Station in Georgia (see Appendix).

The seeds tend to take a long time to germinate, and bottom heating is the key to speeding up the process. The *chinense*, being tropical plants, do best in areas with high humidity and warm nights, but we have heard reports of *chinense* varieties growing well in such diverse locations as northern California, Texas, Illinois, and Louisiana. Wherever they are planted, however, they are slow growers, especially in the Southwest, and the growing period is at least one hundred days or more for mature pods. The yield varies enormously according to the varieties grown and how well the particular plants adapt to the local environment; we have grown stunted plants with as few as ten pods and large, bushy plants with fifty or more.

In 1990 we experimented with growing *chinense* in Albuquerque, which, given its dry air and cool summer nights, does not have an ideal environment. Dave grew four different varieties of *chinense* from Belize, Jamaica, Costa Rica, and Cuba in pots and they all did poorly. However, the same varieties grew slowly but yielded many more fruits in the garden.

In 1993, however, Dave had more success growing the peppers in pots. He used larger pots and a much looser soil mixture containing milled spaghnum moss. Also, he placed the pots in partial shade so that they only received full sun in the early morning and late afternoon. The yields were large, with some of the bigger potted plants producing more than forty pods.

The garden-planted varieties for 1993 grew only half as large as the potted *chinenses*, and their yields were very low. We discussed the situation with Paul Bosland, and he suggested that it was probably caused by a soil condition in the DeWitt garden that the *chinense* just didn't like. In the next garden, Dave is going to set aside a special section for *chinense* and loosen the soil mixture considerably. It seems that the *chinenses* are particularly sensitive to compacted soil.

Preserving the Heat

Over the years, many people have asked us how to preserve the habanero crop. The simplest method is simply to wash and dry the pods and place them in a plastic bag in the freezer. They will lose some of their firmness when defrosted, but the flavor, heat, and aroma are all preserved. Habaneros can be puréed with a little vinegar, and the mixture will keep in the refrigerator for weeks. They can also be pickled or turned into sauces (see pages 41–58). Another common preservation method is drying the pods. They should be cut in half vertically and placed in a food dehydrator. After they are thoroughly dried, they can be stored in jars, stored in plastic bags in the freezer, or ground into powders. Drying does not affect the heat level of the pods, but pods that are rehydrated lose some flavor and aroma.

Brazil and Beyond

The chiltepin (*C. annuum* var. *aviculare*) is generally thought to be the wild progenitor of the rest of the *annuum* species. Put another way, the undomesticated and primitive chiltepins are the original genetic material from which the cultivated varieties we know today evolved through human selection. Since the *annuum* species has a wild progenitor, it makes sense that the *chinense* species would have one, too. The trouble is, no one's certain of this. "So far the wild progenitor has not been discovered," states J. W. Purseglove in his book, *Spices*.

But maybe it has been discovered. Just as there are people who collect stamps or trading cards, there are professionals and hobbyists who collect seeds. Chile seeds, to be more specific, and *chinense* seeds to narrow the focus even further. Jim Ault is such a person. At Longwood Gardens in Kennett Square, Pennsylvania, he maintains a collection of about one hundred *Capsicum* accessions (varieties) of which forty are *chinense*. His offer to swap seed with us in 1993 was gratefully accepted, and we sent off seed that we had collected in Trinidad and Costa Rica. Jim was generous in return, sending us six *chinense* varieties from Africa, Bolivia, Peru, Cuba, and Brazil.

We already had two Brazilian *chinense* in our collection, so we felt that the plants from Jim's seed would make an interesting comparison. The specimen of Jim's unnamed Brazilian *chinense* that was planted in the garden did poorly, but its counterpart flourished in a large pot, growing two feet tall and two and a half feet wide. The leaves, though only an inch long, had the characteristic crinkled aspect found in the *chinense*, and the fruits ranged from one to three per node. And what fruits they were!

Instead of the familiar lantern shape of many *chinense*, these were spherical, upright pods about one-quarter inch wide. It was the smallest-podded *chinense* we'd ever encountered. The pods' resemblance to the Sonoran chiltepins was startling; they were nearly identical—with one exception. Instead of being red, the mature Brazilian pods were bright yellow. We performed the smell test by cutting a pod in half and discovered the unmistakable, apricotlike aroma of the *chinense*. It was so pungent that when we held it close to our noses, we were convulsed by fits of sneezing. We also noticed that the pods were not easily deciduous or, in other words, they did not separate easily from the calyx like the chiltepin pods.

The two other Brazilian varieties we grew out in 1993 were *aji yaquitania* and *pimenta do cheiro*, both from seed provided by F. P. Williamson of Cambridge, Maryland, who travels to Brazil frequently on business. The *aji yaquitania* produced orange, pendant, football-shaped pods about ¾ inch long and ⅜ inch wide. Interestingly enough, that variety has overwintered successfully in our cool, north-exposed greenhouse even though other *chinenses* have not survived.

Pimenta do cheiro is a variety with a number of variant spellings, including *pimento de cheiro*. Apparently, it has a number of pod shapes as well, since its name means "odiferous pepper," which could apply to any of the *chinense*. H. Nagai of the Instituto Agronomico de Campinas in Brazil lists *pimenta de cheiro* as one of three cultivated *chinense* varieties in the country, along with *murici* and *pimenta-de-bode*. W. B. Mars and Carlos Rizzini, authors of *Useful Plants of Brazil*, describe *pimenta de cheiro* as "roundish yellow fruits the size of a grape, which are highly aromatic."

That description matched the *aji yaquitania* variety more closely than our *pimenta do cheiro*, which had red pods an inch long and ⅜ inch wide that resembled a miniature serrano. They grew both horizontally and partially upright, and they had a thin pod wall, which caused the fruits to dry out quickly. They were, however, highly aromatic. It is likely that, considering the diversity of pod shapes of the Brazilian *chinense*, this odiferous pepper appears in many forms.

"The Amazon basin supports the world's largest number of habanero varieties," notes Jessica Harris, the author of *Tasting Brazil*. "These chiles appear in a variety of ways in Brazilian cooking, particularly that of the northeastern region. They are chopped and put into homemade sauces and pickled and show up on the table as condiments."

Interestingly enough, in the Amazon region of Brazil, mildly pungent *chinense* varieties have been crossed with bell peppers to produce sweet hybrids that are more disease-resistant than *annuums* under hot and humid conditions. S.S. Cheng, the researcher responsible for the experiment, wrote: "The advantages of *C. chinense* cultivation are the longer harvest periods, no pesticide application requirement, and low production cost. A breeding program is under way to transfer fruit quality from *C. annuum* to *C. chinense*." The ease with which *chinense* crosses with *annuum* will ensure many hybrids in the future—in Brazil and around the world.

When Columbus first explored the Caribbean islands in 1492, there's a good chance that the first chile pepper he encountered was a Scotch bonnet or its cousin. After all, long before Columbus arrived, the *chinense* had spread throughout the islands, presumably by ancestors of the Arawaks and Caribs. So it would not be surprising to learn that Columbus misnamed the pod *pimiento* (pepper) right after biting into a *chinense*.

According to Jean Andrews, "After 1493, peppers from the West Indies were available to the Portuguese for transport to their western African colonies." Brazilian peppers were available by 1508, when Portugal colonized Brazil. After sugar cane was introduced into Brazil in 1532, there was a great need for slave labor. Considerable trade sprang up between Portuguese colonies in Angola and Mozambique and across the Atlantic in Pernambuco, Brazil. It is believed that this trade introduced New World peppers into Africa, especially the *chinense* and *frutescens* species.

The *chinense* varieties are not a major agricultural crop in Africa. A search of agricultural reports from the chile-growing countries of

Congo pepper seedings at the Botanic Station, Tobago.

Ethiopia, Nigeria, and Liberia revealed that although *annuum* and *frutescens* varieties were listed, *chinense* was not. Perhaps the *chinense* are grown mostly in household plots, much the same way they are in the Yucatán Peninsula.

Our experience with the African *chinenses* is limited to the *fatalii* variety from the Central African Republic, which we grew from seed provided by Jim Ault. The plants grew well both in the garden and in pots, being tall, vigorous growers with high pod yields. The pendant pods started green, matured to bright yellow and—like their name suggests—were deadly hot. They grew with a distinctly pointed end, which was somewhat unusual for a species whose members' pods have mostly rounded or blunt ends.

We were unable to visit Brazil or Africa to witness the *chinense* in their habitats there, but at least we had the pleasure of growing the pods in New Mexico. We did, however, visit quite a few other exotic locales where the *chinense* flourish.

Fiery Origins

The Amazon basin was the center of origin for the *chinense* species, but the story of the spread of the wild varieties and their eventual domestication is still unclear. Supposedly, the oldest known *chinense* specimen ever found was a single intact pod that was discovered in Preceramic levels (6500 BC) in Guitarrero Cave in coastal Peru. Such a discovery considerably predates the generally accepted time of chile pepper cultivation and suggests that the pod was introduced later to the archaeological site, or that by that date wild *chinense* pods had migrated far from their center of origin and had been collected by early hunter-gatherer civilizations.

Since both wild and domesticated forms of the Brazilian *chinense* exist today (there is some debate about the wild varieties), we can assume that the species was domesticated much in the same manner as the *annuum* pepper species was in Mexico. First, it was a tolerated weed with upright-growing ("erect," in botanical terminology) fruits. Then, as humans planted the seeds and tended the plants, there was a gradual evolution to larger pods that hung down from the plant (pendant) as a result of human selection.

The domestication of the *chinense* species occurred around 2000 BC, and, according to ethnobotanist Barbara Pickersgill, "its domestication was probably connected with the development of agriculture in tropical forests. It seems reasonable to assume that *C. chinense* was domesticated east of the Andes by these tropical forest agriculturists, who were probably responsible for the domestication of manioc." She adds, wryly: "As a condiment, the chile pepper probably formed a welcome addition to any diet consisting largely of manioc starch." By about 1000 BC, domesticated *chinese* varieties had spread to the Pacific coast of Peru.

The cultivation of the *chinense* species produced many pod types and varieties. Bernabe Cobo, a naturalist who traveled throughout South America during the early seventeenth century, probably was the first European to study the *chinense* species. He estimated that there were at least forty different pod types of the chiles, "some as large as limes or large plums; others, as small as pine nuts or even grains of wheat, and between the two extremes are many different sizes. No less variety is found in color…and the same difference is found in form and shape."

Chinense was and still is the most important cultivated pepper species east of the Andes in South America. Barbara Pickersgill notes that the fruit characteristics of the species are more variable around the mouth of the Amazon than farther west because of human selection of the pods.

The dispersion of domesticated *chinense* types into the Caribbean and Central America occurred in two different directions. Some *chinense* varieties spread into the isthmus from Colombia and eventually became common in Panama and Costa Rica. But apparently their spread north was halted before they reached the Yucatán Peninsula. Meanwhile, during their great migrations, the ancestors of the Arawaks and Caribs (Caribbean Indians), transferred the *chinense* from the Amazon Basin through Venezuela and into the Caribbean, where pod types subsequently developed on nearly every island. Pickersgill believes that the habanero was "a historic introduction from the West Indies" into Yucatán, completing the *chinense*'s island-hopping encirclement of the Caribbean Sea.

The Caribbean Rim of Fire

The seeds were carried and cultivated by Native Americans as the *chinense* species hopped, skipped, and jumped around the West Indies, forming—seemingly on each island—specifically adapted pod types that are called "land races" of the species. As we have seen, each land race gained a name in each island or country, although the term "Scotch bonnet" is used generically throughout the region. The pods of these land races became the dominant spicy element of the Caribbean, firing up its cuisines—and its legends.

A well-known West Indies folktale describes a Creole woman who loved the fragrant island pods so much that she decided to make a soup out of them. She reasoned that since the Scotch bonnets were so good in other foods, a soup made exclusively of them would be heavenly. But when her children tasted the broth, it was so blisteringly hot that they ran to the river to cool their mouths. Unfortunately, they drank so much water that they drowned—heavenly, indeed! The moral of the story is to be careful with Scotch bonnets and their relatives, which is why many sauce companies combine them with vegetables or fruits to dilute the heat.

A Caribbean natural pepper remedy supposedly will spice up your love life. In Guadeloupe, where *chinense* is called *le derriere de Madame Jacques*, that pepper is combined with crushed peanuts, cinnamon sticks, nutmeg, vanilla beans packed in brandy, and an island liqueur called Creme de Banana to make an aphrodisiac. We assume it's taken internally.

Caribbean Hot Sauces

An old island adage says that the best Caribbean hot sauce is the one that burns a hole in the tablecloth. We've never seen that happen in all our trips to the Caribbean, but we're certain that the earliest hot sauces in the region were made with the crushed *chinense* varieties. According to some sources, the Carib and Arawak Indians used pepper juice for seasoning, and after the Europeans "discovered" chile peppers, slave ship captains coming from Africa combined pepper juice with palm oil, flour, and water to make a "slabber sauce" that was served over ground beans to the slaves aboard ship.

The most basic hot sauces on the islands have traditionally been made by soaking chopped Scotch bonnets in vinegar and then sprinkling the fiery vinegar on foods. Over the centuries, each island developed its own style of hot sauce by combining the crushed chiles with other ingredients such as mustard, fruits, or tomatoes.

Homemade hot sauces are still common on the islands of the Caribbean. The sauces *piquante* and *chien* from Martinique and *ti-malice* from Haiti all combine shallots, lime juice, garlic, and the hottest *chinenses* available. Puerto Rico has two hot sauces of note: one is called *pique* and is made with acidic Seville oranges and habaneros; the other is *sofrito*, which combines small piquins ("bird peppers") with annatto seeds, cilantro, onions, garlic, and tomatoes. In Jamaica, Scotch bonnets are combined with the pulp and juices of mangoes, papayas, and tamarinds. The Virgin Islands have a concoction known as "asher," which is a corruption of "limes ashore." It combines limes with habaneros, cloves, allspice, salt, vinegar, and garlic.

Another good example of the combination of habaneros and other ingredients is Melinda's (called Marie Sharp's Hot Sauce in the United States), made in Belize from habaneros, carrots, and onions, which makes for a milder, more flavorful sauce than simply combining the puréed chiles with vinegar.

Jamaica's Pickapeppa sauce has a flavor similar to Worcestershire sauce and only a slight bite. Its fruity flavor comes from mangoes, raisins, and tamarind. However, it should be noted that the company also sells a much hotter version of Pickapeppa with more Scotch bonnets and less fruit.

Another famous Caribbean hot sauce is Barbados Jack, which has been produced by the Miller family of Barbados since 1965. It consists of Bonney peppers, mustard, turmeric, and onions, and is commonly served over seafood and poultry dishes. According to Caribbean expert Chelle Koster Walton, "The Millers began by selling ladlesful to neighborhood customers at the rate of thirty gallons a week. Eventually the Millers poured their sauce into recycled soda bottles and rum flasks, and distributed them around town by bicycle." In the late 1980s, their production was up to 1,900 gallons of Barbados Jack *a week*.

The hot sauce called Matouk's owes its existence to a speech by Trinidadian political leader Dr. Eric Williams, who said that the variety of jams, jellies, sauces, and pickles made by housewives were an integral part of Trinidad's culture. However, he pointed out that as women gained employment, the nation was in danger of losing the tastes of the home kitchens of Trinidad and Tobago. George Matouk, a Trinidadian businessman, was inspired by Williams's speech, and in 1968 he founded Matouk's Food Products and began manufacturing traditional-style jams, jellies, and hot sauces. To make the hot sauce, which is available in three heat levels, Congo peppers (the local name for habaneros) are combined with herbs, spices, and papayas. About half of the Matouk's sauce production is consumed locally, and the rest is exported, with the United States as the number-one market for Matouk's Trinidadian hot sauces.

Trinidad and Tobago: Congo Peppers and More

While exploring the multifaceted cuisines of Trinidad and Tobago (T&T), Dave and his wife, Mary Jane, had the opportunity to experience Congo pepper fever on those two islands. In Trinidad, "Congo" means anything large and powerful, and this type of *chinense* lives up to its name. We found some as large as lemons, and they had thicker walls than most of the habaneros we were familiar with.

Our hosts and guides in Trinidad were Marie Permenter and Vernon and Irene Montrichard, who own thirteen Royal Castle fried chicken restaurants on Trinidad. What makes their chicken different from Kentucky Fried Chicken, the competition, is that it is marinated in a sauce made from Congo peppers and a number of fresh herbs (Spanish and French thyme, mostly) that are grown in the nearby hills of Paramin. They also export this hot-sauce base is exported to Jacksonville Beach, Florida, where it is manufactured into Trinidad Habanero Sauce by Caribbean Food Products.

Marie and Vernon took us on a tour to their Congo pepper fields and introduced us to the growers, who lived in a nearby shack. The well-established planting was several acres in size and was surrounded by thick vegetation. We learned that the Congo pepper plants grow about three feet high in a single year and are picked twice. Then they are plowed and the site is replanted. The growers told us that the plants would live for decades, but would produce smaller fruits each year.

We also met up with Congo peppers in Tobago. Scarborough, the capital, has a small but interesting Botanic Station, where we met with Reginald Phillips, the technical officer in charge. He told us that one of the station's main projects was raising Congo pepper seedlings to supply small farmers. Evidence of his efforts was widespread at the market downtown, where vendors sold the brightly colored pods in plastic bags.

Nobody seemed to know exactly how many acres were in pepper production in T&T, but after talking to a few knowledgeable people, like Vernon Montrichard, the figure of two thousand acres seemed to be the best estimate. Much of this crop is exported. Total exports to Canada, the United States, and the United Kingdom amounted to TT$1.6 million in 1991 (equivalent to about U.S. $250,000), with about 131 tons alone to the United States.

The rest of the crop is sold in markets and is used to make hot sauces. Every family in T&T seemingly has its own recipe, but the plethora of homemade sauces has not prevented a large hot sauce industry from springing up. There are perhaps five major manufacturers of hot sauce in T&T and about ten minor ones. The best known T&T hot sauces sold in the United States are the Matouk's hot sauces and the Trinidad Habanero Sauce, which we described earlier.

Jamaica: Scotch Bonnets and Country Peppers

"In Jamaica, much use is made of fresh peppers," writes Norma Benghiat, author of *Traditional Jamaican Cookery*, "the most highly esteemed hot pepper being the 'Scotch bonnet', which has a wonderful perfume and flavour." She adds, tantalizingly: "In recent times a Scotch bonnet pepper has been developed which retains the aroma and flavour, but is not hot." According to another source, this mystery pepper, also called "seasoning pepper," is mildly pungent and remains green, never maturing to orange or red.

We tried to track down this pepper during several trips to Jamaica, and at first we thought we had found it: the "country pepper," as it's called. But the more we asked people to distinguish among the varieties, the more we became caught up in a confusion over names.

According to vendor Bernice Campbell in the Ocho Rios market, country peppers are more elongated than Scotch bonnets, and have more flavor. With a typical pepper contrariness, cook Betty Wilson disagrees. While serving us fricasséed chicken and grilled parrot fish at a streamside picnic on the Rio Grande near Port Antonio, she claimed that Scotch bonnets are not as hot as country peppers but are more "flavored." Our room attendant at Ciboney Resort, however, insisted that no, Scotch bonnets *were* hotter than country peppers. And habanero grower Graham Jacks wrote to us that "one of these country peppers is a deep brownish purple when ripe, and is truly ferociously hot; much hotter than the Scotch bonnet."

To add to the confusion, a variety called Jamaican Hot occasionally appears in pepper literature. Author and chef Mark Miller, in his guide *The Great Chile Book*, describes it as "smaller than the habanero but similar in shape." It is possible that this variety is the same as the West Indian Hot mentioned by Jean Andrews, but pepper importer Joe Litwin told us that the "hots" are generic terms used in the United States but not in Jamaica.

According to Litwin, who imports Jamaican peppers through his KAL International Company, there are two kinds of Scotch bonnet: One is green and matures to yellow; it is very common and is usually called Scotch bonnet. The other is a red pepper in the same shape, which is termed "country pepper." Large, red, habanero-shaped pods are also called country pepper and are probably Congo pepper imports from Trinidad.

A search of the 1994 edition of *Seed Savers Yearbook* revealed common names of cultivated varieties to be Jamaica Large Red, Jamaica Orange, Jamaica Small Red, and the appellation Scotch bonnet with the descriptors "orange," "yellow," and "red" added. Not surprisingly, we remain confused about country peppers, seasoning peppers and Jamaica hots, but we have solved the country pepper mystery. On a subsequent trip to Jamaica, our guide David Brown told us that it would be confusing to ask Jamaicans to compare country peppers with Scotch bonnets because "Scotch bonnets are country peppers but not all country peppers are

Scotch bonnets." That momentarily baffled us, but he continued, "Country pepper is just a general term for garden peppers. Any cultivated pepper is a country pepper. That term distinguishes them from black pepper or pepper sauce."

Joe Litwin, incidentally, started growing Scotch bonnets in Jamaica in 1991; he had previously cultivated organic sugar cane. He has twenty-five acres under cultivation in various parts of Jamaica and he also utilizes contract fields. There is no way to estimate total Jamaican production, Joe told us, but his company imports the fresh pods into the United States at the rate of three to four thousand pounds a week, and because of fears of drug loads being smuggled along with the peppers, Joe or one of his employees personally oversees the loading of every shipment of Scotch bonnets onto the plane. He also manufactures a line of products under the Jabeba House house brand, including Scotch Bonnet hot sauces in red and yellow, and jerk sauce.

Jerk Sauces

Jamaican jerk sauces are a combination of spices and Scotch bonnet chiles used as a marinade and baste for grilled meats (we offer our favorite jerk sauce recipes on pages 93–110). The word "jerk" is thought to have originated from the word "ch?arki" (the question mark is part of the word), a Quecha word from Peru. The Spanish converted the term to "charqui," which meant jerked, or dried, meat, which, in English, became known as "jerk" and "jerky."

The technique of jerking was originated by the Maroons, Jamaican slaves who escaped from the British during the invasion of 1655 and hid in the maze of jungles and limestone sinkholes known as the Cockpit Country. The Maroons seasoned their pork and cooked it until it was dry and would preserve well in the humidity of the tropics. During the twentieth century, the technique gained popularity in Jamaica and today "jerk pork shacks" are commonly found all over the island. The method has evolved, however, and the pork is no longer overcooked. In addition to pork, heavily spiced chicken, fish, and beef are grilled to juicy perfection. Dozens of brands of jerk sauces are manufactured both in Jamaica and the United States.

Yucatán: Land of the Habanero

The Yucatán Peninsula juts into the Caribbean Sea like a beacon, attracting lovers of the hottest peppers in the world. We, too, have succumbed to Yucatán's lure, and have returned there often to sample its delights. In 1985, Nancy and Jeff, Nancy's husband, made their first trip to Belize, where they discovered Melinda's Hot Sauce with its original yellow label of three red habanero chiles. That was the first year Marie Sharp had it on the market—she started at the beginning of the year and Nancy and Jeff were there in the fall. They came back with their suitcases full of the sauce, and everyone they knew got a bottle as a gift. When they returned to Belize during the 1988 Christmas holidays with Dave and Mary Jane, everybody was looking to replenish their stock.

The DeWitts and the Gerlachs set up headquarters in the town of San Pedro on Ambergris Cay, northeast of Belize City. Although the primary purposes of our visit were diving, snorkeling, and fishing, we soon became fascinated by the extremely hot sauces produced there that utilized habanero chiles—including Habanero Five Drops, Pica Rico, Hi-Taste, and, of course, Melinda's. At least one bottled sauce was on every restaurant table on the island. We also spotted a habanero plant near our lodgings. Something hot was going on in Belize.

We made some inquiries, and by coincidence it turned out that the habanero plant was being cultivated by our pilot and landlord, Mandy Castillo. We asked Mandy if he knew anything about the hot sauce business in Belize. He laughed and made a phone call. Soon he returned and said that if we paid for the gas, he would fly us to the Maya Mountains and the hot sauce capital of the country. How could we pass up an offer like that?

We dropped our scuba gear and fishing rods for a day and soon were flying over the barrier reef and cays along the coast of Belize. After about forty-five minutes in the air, we landed at the air strip in the tiny town of Melinda in the heart of the vast groves of oranges, mangoes, papayas, and passion fruits. There we were met by Marie and Gerry Sharp, a genial couple who gave us a guided tour of their plantation and the Melinda's Hot Sauce bottling operation.

Marie Sharp began bottling Melinda's Hot Sauce in 1983 after she became frustrated with the prices paid for peppers at the local produce markets. A lover of habanero chiles, she had grown about a hundred plants among citrus groves on the Sharp's four-hundred-acre plantation. After the initial harvest, she carried the chiles to the local market, where buyers insulted her by offering her a paltry $1 Belize (50 cents U.S.) for a *gallon* of pods.

"I will not give away my peppers," Marie vowed, and from that point on she knew that a bottled sauce was the answer to marketing her habaneros. But there was one problem—her friends told her that the other habanero sauces were so hot that a single bottle often lasted six months or more. Since she wanted her customers to buy more than two bottles of sauce a year, Marie began experimenting with numerous recipes in order to find one that offered more flavor and less heat than the competition—in fact, one that would be perfect for export to the chile-hungry U.S. market.

After months of experimentation, Marie developed a recipe that uses cooked vegetables such as carrots and onions as a base, and then adds puréed raw habaneros until the proper heat level is reached. Thus, the Melinda's brand is thicker and more flavorful than the other Belizean habanero sauces, which contain only chiles and vinegar.

Next Marie needed to find a dependable source for the habanero chiles, since she could not grow a sufficient quantity herself. The Sharps contacted various growers and began horticultural experimentation with the habaneros, which, like other peppers, are susceptible to viral diseases in the tropics where the rainfall can be one hundred inches a year or more. In order to standardize color in habaneros, which can vary from orange to purple at maturity, only the reddest pods are selected, and those seeds are spaced for plants three feet apart in rows four feet apart.

By 1988, the Sharps had about five acres of habaneros under cultivation. It took about seven pounds of peppers to produce about five gallons of hot sauce at that time, and the Melinda's operation was bottling three hundred to four hundred cases per month, with forty-eight five-ounce bottles in a case. The sauce was entirely handmade and hand-bottled by fourteen employees overseen by Marie and her foreman, Joe, who personally performed the final taste-test on each batch.

Since our visit to Belize, a legal dispute arose concerning the trade-marked name "Melinda's" on the hot sauce, so Marie now sells her hot sauce under the name of Marie Sharp's here in the United States. (Outside of the United States it is still known as Melinda's.)

Mexico also shares the Yucatán Peninsula, and the story of the habanero there has as much to do with distinctions of class as it does with heat and aroma. The habanero is beloved by the indigenous Maya, who look down their noses at jalapeños and serranos. But on the other hand, so the story goes, the Mexicans of European descent dislike the habanero and regard it as a lowly Mayan pepper with too much perfume. Amal Naj, who traveled in Yucatán while researching his book *Peppers*, noted: "I quickly sensed that the habanero in a way symbolized for the Maya their fierce independence within Mexico and that the jalapeño symbolized the European Mexican, the invader." In reality, of course, the jalapeño is probably the older pepper variety in Mexico, since it was developed in prehistoric times; many experts believe that the habanero is a fairly recent introduction.

In modern Mayan communities, backyard habanero plots are associated with nearly every household, where they often grow as perennial plants. There is some commercial growing; about five hundred farmers grow habaneros on a scant six hundred acres in the Mexican part of the Yucatán Peninsula. About 2,500 tons of fresh pods are harvested each year, and 75 percent of that is used in fresh form, mostly combined into a salsa with lime juice and salt as the salsa Xnipec (see page 50). Twenty-two percent percent of the crop is processed into sauces and the remaining 3 percent is used for seed. The pods are graded according to weight, with the first category weighing over 10 grams, the second 7.5 to 10 grams, and the third 5.0 to 7.5 grams.

Habanero field in Stonewall, Texas.

Severe problems with the habanero crop occurred during the 1970s, with sickly, poor-yielding plants. The problem was finally traced to poor seed—the farmers were using their poorest, unmarketable pods as their seed source. Ordoñez Pool, an agricultural official in the city of Uxmal, collected the best pods he could find and began a breeding process to save the habaneros from extinction. Pool and his associates developed two varieties, Uxmal and INIA, which were released in 1981 using selection for desirable characteristics such as increased yield, orange color, and pungency.

The Uxmal variety yields 47 percent more than native habaneros grown in the same area, and likes reddish soil. It produces three fruits per node. INIA also yields 47 percent more than regional peppers, likes rocky soil, and yields four fruits per node. During Nancy and Jeff's visits to the Mexican Yucatán, they could not distinguish between the two varieties in the markets. They just noticed the typical lantern shape, orange color, and fruity perfume.

The Mexican portion of Yucatán has been physically isolated from the rest of Mexico and the Americas for centuries, surrounded on three sides by water and in the south by dense jungles. After Mexico's independence in 1812 it was more than a hundred years before a peace treaty was signed in territory of Quintana Roo (1935), and it wasn't until 1974 that this area became a state. It was only in the 1960s that a road was cut through the jungle to link the area with the rest of Mexico! So although it is a part of Mexico, Yucatán has preserved a cuisine that is distinct from the rest of the country. In fact, the presence of Europeans has little impact on the cuisine, which is almost purely Mayan. It is interesting to see the role that chiles, namely habaneros, play in traditional Mayan dishes.

Salsas are common in Mexico and are popular in this area. Most of them are served very fresh, almost as if they are prepared individually for each customer. One thing you can always count on when eating in Mexico is that there will be a bowl of salsa or a bottle of hot sauce available. An extremely popular and surprising salsa ingredient, although certainly not unique, is the red radish. Markets in Yucatán are full of big, beautiful, hot red radishes, and although their use in salsas now seems logical to us, it was quite surprising at first to see them combined with habaneros in a hot salsa (see page 48).

The most famous seasonings from Yucatán are the *recados*, pastes that are made from spices and herbs such as cinnamon, allspice, black pepper, oregano, cumin, black peppercorns, annatto seeds, and cloves, along with habaneros and garlic. These unique pastes were developed by the Maya long before the arrival of the Spaniards and are the basis for some of the most popular dishes in Yucatán, including *pollo pibil,* chicken that is covered with *recado* seasoning, wrapped in banana leaves and cooked in a pit—in a manner that dates back to pre-Columbian times.

The Mayas do not cook much with the habanero chile, but it is always present in their salsas. It is more of a personal choice that way, and one can add the heat to suit their own taste. For example, in the Mayan recipe for Campeche Shrimp Cocktail (see page 69), the chopped habanero is served as an accompaniment to be added as desired. The Maya love to roast habaneros, then slice and serving them as a condiment for such dishes as *cochinita pibi* (spiced pork steamed in banana leaves).

The Story of Rica Red

In September 1992, the DeWitts and Gerlachs accepted the invitation of Stuart Jeffrey and Cody Jordan of Quetzál Foods to visit their habanero plantation in Costa Rica. They were growing a variety they called Rica Red on about two hundred acres in the northern part of the country.

After an evening of relaxation streamside at the Tilajari Hotel Resort, within sight of the highly active Arenal Volcano, we continued our journey north, and Stuart and Cody explained how they started growing habaneros in Costa Rica. Their story was a classic tale of determination and problem solving. It all began in 1984, when Stuart, who had been an agronomist working with kiwi fruit, began growing habaneros in New Orleans from seeds he brought back from his native Belize. His fascination with the fiery and tasty habaneros led to dreams of producing habanero products, but he needed adequate production. He investigated buying a couple of sauce plants in Belize, but they were just too small to be feasible.

By this time he had contacted his longtime friend Cody, and had sent him a sauce he had concocted from his backyard habaneros, plus some dried pods and powder. Cody took these fledgling products around Dallas to restaurants and spice companies. Although no one had ever heard of habaneros, the response was overwhelming. One restaurant wanted a hundred cases of hot sauce immediately. One spice company placed an order for two million pounds of habanero powder! It was clear they could not fill those orders from Stuart's backyard garden and that they had to locate massive amounts of habaneros. But where?

Stuart and Cody began searching the Caribbean and Central America for the ideal spot to find (or grow) large quantities of habaneros. Some were grown in the Yucatán Peninsula of Mexico, but that crop was consumed locally and was not exported. They explored Guatemala, Honduras, the Dominican Republic, Dominica, and Jamaica and found the same situation everywhere—small plots with limited commercial habanero production. In 1985, somewhat discouraged but not ready to give up, they posted bulletins with the Foreign Agricultural Service of U.S. Embassies in Central America: PEPPER GROWERS WANTED!

Finally, a response came from Ricardo Quieros of the University of Costa Rica. He could help them, he wrote, and his family had grown peppers for many years. That was the break Stuart and Cody needed. They rushed to Costa Rica and inspected Ricardo's ten acres of a *panameño*/cayenne cross. Ricardo told them it was not a true habanero, but that one could be developed.

The next few years were devoted to developing the Rica Red habanero variety and determining where to grow it. Ricardo collected seeds from Centro Agronomico de Investigacion y Ensenanza (CATIE) and twenty-two varieties of *panameño* peppers being grown on two small plots in Limón and planted them on sites all around the country—isolated, of course, from other varieties of peppers. From those plantings, Ricardo selected six strains which had desirable qualities: large, round pods, bright red color, high heat, and disease resistance. These strains were again planted around the country, and the seeds from the best pods were collected. Finally, after four years, Ricardo had the Rica Red variety breeding true more than 90 percent of the time and had determined the ideal spot to grow it. The location was the northernmost town in Costa Rica, and it is called, appropriately enough, Los Chiles.

Stuart and Cody estimated that they and their Costa Rican partners have invested about $1.5 million in the Rica Red habanero operation, creating jobs for the locals and hot pods for American consumers in the process. The Rica Red habaneros were fermented in mash form in a plant at the site, and the mash was sold to Louisiana hot sauce manufacturers to spice up their cayenne sauces.

Since we visited Los Chiles, Stuart and Cody have expanded their operation, which means that habanero imports are up, increasing the United States's balance of chiles deficit, which hit $51.5 million in 1992. But American habanero farmers are fighting back!

The U.S. Invasion: More Powerful Than Killer Bees

How is it that an obscure pepper like the habanero became the chile of choice in the United States in about a decade? To answer that question, we have searched what little literature is available on the subject, interviewed habaneroheads, and traveled to the centers of habanero culture in this country.

A Brief but Hot History

Although the *chinense* variety known as the datil pepper has been grown near St. Augustine, Florida, for hundreds of years (see below), the other varieties of the species were virtually unknown in this country until quite recently. The first detailed discussion of the species appeared in the *Bulletin of the Torrey Botanical Club* in 1957. Botanists Paul G. Smith and Charles B. Heiser, Jr. (who spelled the species "*sinense*") wrote that they collected seeds for ten years in order to study the species and eventually grew plants from eight-five different lots of seed at the University of California, Davis and Indiana University. They wrote that the smallest-podded plants they grew came from British Guiana (now Guyana).

At the time that Smith and Heiser were writing, the only habanero products in the United States were the occasional bottles of Caribbean hot sauces brought back by tourists—except for one domestic product, Scotch Bonnet, a sherry-pepper sauce. Amazingly enough, this first U.S.-made habanero product goes back more than a century. Pepper sauce manufacturer Louis Borie, of Richmond, Vermont, tells the story: "My family has been producing Scotch Bonnet for more than one hundred years. As best as I can determine, my great-great grandfather began making the product for himself and, eventually, some friends in the Philadelphia area. My grandfather started selling it through John Wagner and Sons some time in the early part of the century. My father continued to make the product for Wagner's, and when he died several years ago, I took over production.

"Wagner's has never made much of an effort to market the product outside of the Philadelphia area, probably because they assumed there was little market for it. Consequently, production has been limited, although I know my grandfather did make it in some quantity in the thirties and forties. I am making more of an effort to market the product now that peppers and hot foods have become more popular.

"My family has always grown the Scotch bonnets in the Philadelphia area and now in Vermont. The pepper seed has apparently been in our family since my ancestors emigrated from France to the United States by way of Haiti in the early 1800s. The story is that they had to flee Haiti during a slave uprising and managed to take a few pepper seeds with them."

The next habanero products available commercially in the United States were hot sauces imported in the 1970s. It is quite difficult to track down the precise dates when regular importation of the various *chinense*-containing sauces began, but we do know that in the early 1970s, Matouk's Hot Sauce from Trinidad was imported into the United States through Brooklyn, New York, and two versions of Jamaica's Pickapeppa (one mild, one quite hot) began appearing in U.S. groceries.

Interest in the habanero and its cousins was piqued in 1984, when Jean Andrews described the species in her book *Peppers: The Domesticated Capsicums.* "This is the chili pepper that separates the men from the boys," she wrote, and portrayed it as the "secret weapon" of Louisiana pepper-eating contests.

It is difficult to determine which of the U.S. datil sauces was the first on the market, but we do know that Chris Way was packaging his Dat'l Do It in 1981 (see pages 30–31). Other datil sauces of the 1980s included Liquid Summer, manufactured by blues musician Bill Wharton, and Salsa del Diablo, made by Jeff Campbell and only sold from his roadside stand in Stonewall, Texas.

In 1988, fresh habaneros appeared at the first National Fiery Foods Show held in El Paso, Texas, when Jeff brought fresh pods from his farm (no habanero products were displayed at the show). About the same time, Chris Schlesinger of the East Coast Grill in Cambridge, Massachusetts, began mixing Scotch bonnets with onions, mustard, and tropical fruit juices. The result was his Inner Beauty hot sauce, a brand that soon became very popular.

During the next few years, as habanero sauces and other products were introduced, the most common reader questions, phone calls, and recipe requests to the *Chile Pepper* magazine concerned habaneros. "Continually, people call our office looking for fresh habaneros, habanero sauces, and habanero seeds from this powerful chile," wrote Robert Spiegel, publisher of *Chile Pepper*, in 1989. Robert del Grande, owner and chef of Cafe Annie's in Houston, recalls that, in the late 1980s, "We would pay top dollar to get them [habaneros] from the Caribbean. Half would be rotten, garbage material, and the other half were past their prime."

Then, at the second National Fiery Foods Show in 1990 in Albuquerque, Nancy and Jeff gave little pieces of pickled habaneros to friends they knew could take the heat or those who were so macho that nothing seemed even warm to them at the show. These proved to be very popular.

At the time, Melinda's Hot Sauce from Belize (see pages 21–22) became the fastest-selling hot sauce introduced in this country. The sauce was so popular that it transcended the specialty food market and was soon available in supermarkets nationwide. It proved to be the leader for the popularization of habanero products, which soon proliferated. Additionally, Frieda's Finest (now, Frieda's, Inc.), a California specialty produce company, began nationwide distribution of dried habaneros to supermarkets on May 4, 1990. The success of the dried product led to the distribution of fresh habaneros in September of the same year. Another specialty produce company, Melissa's World Variety Produce, soon began distributing a variety called goat pepper, a *chinense* with a presumably Bahamian origin.

At the 1991 National Fiery Foods Show in Albuquerque, there were at least ten habanero products on display—both imported and domestic—which included hot sauces, marinades, and jerk sauces. The jerk sauces, based on Jamaican recipes (see pages 93–110), reflected the growing appeal of Caribbean foods; most contained Scotch bonnet or habanero variety chiles, pimento (allspice, not to be confused with pimiento, the olive-stuffing pepper), onions, and salt. Other ingredients commonly added included garlic, ginger, vinegar, soy sauce, ketchup, thyme, cinnamon, and nutmeg.

By the end of 1994, at least twelve national seed companies were carrying generic habanero seed, *Seed Saver's Exchange Yearbook* listed the availability of seed from approximately fifty *chinense* varieties, and the fresh pods began appearing with more regularity in supermarkets in Arizona, Texas, and other states. One mail-order catalog contained thirty-four different habanero sauces.

We attempted to find out the total number of habanero sauces by asking Chip Hearn of Dewey Beach, Delaware, who has the world's largest hot sauce collection—more than two thousand different kinds. He said that "hundreds and hundreds" of them were habanero sauces and laughed when we asked for an exact count.

Whatever the number of habanero products, no one doubts their growing popularity, which parallels the overall trend toward hot and spicy foods in this country. And the enormous demand for habaneros in particular has led to habanero farming in the United States.

Datil Do It

Imagine a chile-growing operation so secure that it even has a watch alligator on guard! That's the Dat'l Do It high-tech operation underway in St. Augustine, Florida—even though head datil Chris Way admits that the seven-foot gator is a peaceful (so far) resident of the adjacent lake that supplies the irrigation water for the project.

Chris is growing datil peppers to supply his business of manufacturing datil-based products. His dependence on contract growers had been risky because if they ever refused to grow the datils, Chris realized that his manufacturing business would be doomed.

But why would anyone want to grow this oddly named pepper (*datil* is Spanish for "edible date"), anyway? Well, datils have a long and honorable history in St. Augustine. For centuries they have been associated with northeast Florida's Minorcan community, which arrived in the New World in 1768. There are two scenarios for the datil's introduction into Florida. The first holds that datil seeds were transferred from Brazil to Portugal by early explorers, and from there spread—via birds and traders—throughout Africa and the Mediterranean, in particular to the island of Minorca, off the coast of Spain. The Minorcans became inordinately fond of these peppers, the story goes, and brought the seeds with them when they emigrated to Florida, thus reintroducing them into the New World.

The second—and most likely—scenario suggests that datils were already in Florida when the Minorcans arrived and were brought there from the West Indies by Spanish traders and settlers who traveled the Caribbean. No matter how they arrived, though, Chris Way has cornered the market on these hot little pods.

In 1981, Chris opened Barnacle Bill's restaurant in St. Augustine and made a hot datil-pepper sauce to serve with his fish and other seafood specialties. Each table had its own jar of Dat'l Do It sauce, but they began disappearing at an alarming rate. Chris soon realized that his best customers were *stealing* the bottles of hot sauce. Far from being upset, he reasoned that they *had* to steal it—because he had never offered it for sale! Chris was then approached by one of his customers, who was a vice president of Wynn-Dixie, a supermarket chain. He liked the Dat'l Do It sauce, he said, and if Chris was willing to improve his packaging, the Wynn-Dixies would carry it. So was born the Dat'l Do It operation, which now has nine products: Dat'l Do It Hot Sauce, Hellish Relish, and chile-flavored mustards, vinegars, and jellies. Chris also has a retail Dat'l Do It shop in the tourist district of St. Augustine.

The Dat'l Do It products need a bountiful supply of datils, and that's where the growing operation fits in to the scheme of things. They are grown in pots on elevated platforms, so the pickers (who are surfers recruited from nearby beaches) don't have to bend over. Chris's goal is eventually to grow fifty thousand pounds of datils a year to supply his burgeoning hot sauce business.

Red habaneros ready for processing.

A Habanero Grows in Stonewall

The last time we visited Jeff Campbell, a habanero farmer in Stonewall, in the heart of the Texas Hill Country, his 1993 harvest was underway. Bushel baskets of the bright orange habaneros ringed the plots as the pickers sweated in the hundred-degree weather. The baskets were loaded onto pickups and carried back to Jeff's roadside stand. There the pods were washed, sorted, and readied to be made into some of Jeff's killer Salsa del Diablo.

"It's too hot out here," Jeff complained. "Let's get a beer."

Fortunately, the Stonewall Chili Pepper Company is conveniently located next to Lindig's Bar, so in seconds we were popping the tops off of Lone Star longnecks while Jeff bared his soul about his love affair with the world's hottest chile.

Jeff discovered habaneros in 1980, more than a decade before they became the darlings of American pepper consumers. He was in Terlingua, Texas, at the time, attending the big chili cookoff there, when he met a man who showed him some orange, lantern-shaped peppers that were reputedly the hottest in the world. Jeff tasted the pods and agreed, in tears, that they were, yes, extremely hot and asked where they came from.

"Belize," answered the man, who added that they were impossible to grow in the States because the seeds would not germinate. When Jeff said that he had a pepper farm, the man gave Jeff all his seeds and wished him luck. Thus was born a unique pepper-growing operation.

Jeff soon learned that the trick to germinating habanero seeds was bottom heat and a warm greenhouse. In 1981, he grew a few plants, which he isolated from his other peppers—jalapeños, serranos, tabascos, and some New Mexican varieties.

"At first the people in Stonewall thought I was crazy to be growing habaneros," Jeff told us. Each year thereafter, he increased the number of habanero plants and eventually began selling the pods at this stand and using them in his products, such as salsas. The response from his local customers was overwhelmingly positive, so Jeff continued to expand his habanero production.

By 1992, of Jeff's eighteen acres of peppers, four were planted in habaneros, and he had contracted with a friend to grow plants for his habanero seed in isolation, two miles from any other peppers. In 1993 he expanded his growing to thirty acres, which included sixty thousand habaneros among his total of two hundred thousand plants. He farms out his germination operation to a commercial greenhouse that germinates and grows his seedlings in March in a very warm greenhouse. "Habaneros are tropical plants and they like heat," he says.

Jeff sells the pods fresh, dehydrates some (which he grinds into powder), and is experimenting with smoking them in the fashion of chipotles. But most of the pods are processed into sixteen different Stonewall products, including a habanero paste, jams, ketchup, several salsas, and even lollipops. The habanero lollipops are so hot that few people are able to finish one.

Although he has never calculated his profit per acre, Jeff says that his habanero operation is very profitable and he intends to keep expanding his acreage. One reason for his profitability is that, like Chris Way, Jeff has a retail store where he sells his fresh-market peppers, peaches, and other produce, as well as his products. Also, he moves quite a bit of habanero and other pepper products through his mail-order catalog (see Stonewall Chili Pepper Co. in the Appendix).

Meanwhile, back at Lindig's Bar, Jeff looked tired. He was probably thinking about all the work he had to do, since harvest is by far the busiest time of the year. Or maybe he was thinking about the balance of chiles deficit and how American chile growers had to increase production to fight the glut of foreign peppers. But then he brightened up. "How 'bout some chips and salsa to go along with this Lone Star?" he suggested. "I think I know where to find some."

The Hottest of the Hot: The Story of the Red Savina

When Frank Garcia Jr., first read about habaneros in a magazine article in 1988, he was amazed by the fact that the world's hottest chile pepper was not available in the United States. He began to wonder if a commercial opportunity existed.

You might think that Frank was already a pepper grower, but he wasn't. He was marketing director for an aerospace company. But he was a home gardener, as were his cohorts in the aerospace firm, Frank Neimeyer (now deceased) and John Schermerhorn (now retired). In an astonishingly bold move for three entrenched high-tech engineers, they combined the initials of their last names and formed GNS Spices. Their goal? To astound the skeptics and prove that they could grow habaneros commercially in a nontropical environment in the United States.

They had problems in the beginning. First, hardly anyone had heard of the habanero variety (although Scotch bonnets were fairly well known). So if they grew them, who would buy them? And seeds, where would they get the seeds? In their first year, 1987, they invested $10 in ten packets of habanero seeds from an Oregon seed company—the only ones they could locate. Gleefully, they planted them and waited for the bumper crop of habaneros to come. None of the seeds germinated.

"We were crushed," says Frank. "It was instant failure."

However, the engineers did not give up. They applied the same principles to habanero farming that they did to solving engineering problems. They researched pepper-seed germination and tracked down seed sources. They read everything available on pepper growing (which wasn't much in those days).

The next year was better. The seeds germinated and the partners grew fifty plants. Finally, they had some actual pods to show potential customers. As the marketing partner of the company, Frank decided to hit

the road in 1989 to make sales calls. His success was better than he ever imagined. An East Coast company placed a verbal order for one hundred thousand pounds of habaneros at a good price.

Ecstatic, Frank returned to California and proceeded to figure out how to plant thirty acres of habaneros. First, they had to raise some money, so Frank Neimeyer put up some capital. Frank Garcia tapped into his daughters' college education funds and John Schermerhorn invested some of his retirement money. They got advice from horticulturists, bought commercial seed from Petoseed, and even planted the crop near a river to increase humidity in their fields. Despite their inexperience as farmers, everything worked out splendidly, and by the end of the season they had a bumper crop—even more than the company wanted. Frank called the East Coast company and said he was ready to deliver his one hundred thousand pounds of habaneros. The buyer said he had good news and bad news. The good news was that he would accept delivery; the bad news was that he would only pay half of what he had originally promised because he could buy Indian peppers with a high heat level at a much lower price.

"But we had a deal!" Frank complained.

"You got anything in writing on that?" asked the buyer.

It was quite an introduction to the produce business, and Frank had a knot in his stomach when he wondered what he would tell his wife and daughters about their investment. The three partners got together to ponder their problem. Instead of dumping the crop on the market for far less than its value—a move that would have fixed the price of habaneros artificially low—the partners decided to destroy most of the crop by plowing it under.

Just before he hopped on his tractor to begin the odious task, as Frank tells the tale, "I looked down and saw a strange red pepper that shouldn't have been there." It was a "sport," a mutant red habanero that stood out among the standard orange ones. Frank rescued that one pod from their destroyed crop and saved the seeds.

Frank hedged a bit on plowing under his entire crop. In fact, he saved about a quarter of it and dehydrated the pods. He took some of the dried pods to Karen Caplan of Frieda's, Inc., a Los Angeles specialty produce distributor. It was Frieda's who had introduced the kiwi fruit to the United States, so Frank figured that if anyone could figure out what to do with habaneros, it would be them. He was right.

Karen Caplan loved the habanero and realized its commercial possibilities. She packaged the pods in quarter-ounce bags, printed two easy recipes on the label, and began distributing them to supermarkets. She also did cooking demonstrations at trade shows to prove that habaneros were easy to cook with and were accessible to everyone.

The initial response to the dried habaneros was astonishing. As Frieda's CEO, Frieda Caplan, said, "The excitement generated from both the media and from shoppers themselves has been beyond anything we have ever experienced in all the years [eighteen] we've spent introducing new food experiences to the American public." By the fall of 1990, she was ready to start marketing the fresh pods from Frank's second large crop.

By now Frank realized that the job ahead of him was to educate the public about habaneros. He had to let people know that not only was it possible to grow habaneros domestically, but that he had done it. He advertised and got publicity in *Chile Pepper* and other magazines and has since enjoyed the current boom in hot and spicy foods.

By 1994, GNS Spices had more than one hundred customers for their eight habanero products: fresh pods, brined pods, puréed pods, habanero rings, dried whole pods, powdered pods, and two grades of flaked pods. They've also figured out sequential planting so that the pods don't all ripen at the same time!

And remember that sport, the mutant red pod Frank had rescued? Well, during the time that he was building up his habanero business, Frank was selectively breeding lines that had originated from that single pod. His plan was not only to develop a red pod to complement his orange ones, but also to breed one that stood upright in the field for easier commercial harvesting. Additional benefits of this special breeding would be a thicker pod wall, which means that more oleoresin could be extracted, and more heat—much more heat.

The result, a new variety called Red Savina, was tested for pungency in 1994 by Silliker Laboratories of College Station, Texas, which rated the red habanero at an astonishing 577,000 Scoville Units, believed this to be the hottest commercially grown pepper ever measured. Frank has received a plant variety protection certificate on the Red Savina from the U.S. Department of Agriculture, making it one of the few habanero varieties ever offered such protection.

With his Red Savina, Frank faces the task of reeducating a public that has come to think of habaneros as only orange, but that's not a daunting task for him—after all, his company has rebounded from the 1989 failure. He believes that habaneros are no fad and will ultimately become the chile of choice in the United States—if they aren't already!

Habaneros Tamed (Somewhat)

More Than One Hundred

Fiery Recipes

Regarding the heat levels: Because habaneros and their relatives are called for, cooks can assume that every recipe in this book is hot. Recipes that are truly explosive are labeled "Extremely Hot." Of course, the heat level can be adjusted by varying the number of peppers that are used, or by increasing the amounts of the other ingredients. We recommend removing the seeds and placental tissue, thus decreasing the heat—but this is your decision. Remember that the habaneros themselves vary in heat, so it's a good idea to test the peppers you're using by placing a very tiny sliver on your tongue and then chewing it up. You can vary the amount you use accordingly. Cooks should remember that it's always easier to add heat to foods than to remove it. One strategy, especially when cooking with habaneros, is to use less chile when making the dish and then serve it with a habanero sauce on the side. Another strategy is to place powdered habanero in a shaker to add to meals that don't measure up, pungency-wise.

For the sake of authenticity in the recipes, we call for varieties of the *chinense* species by their common names in the locales where the recipes originated, but in all cases habaneros—both domestic and imported—can be substituted. In fact, any *chinense* variety can be substituted for any other—Scotch bonnets for datil peppers, for example. If you can't find fresh peppers, you may use pickled or reconstituted dried ones, but the flavor will not be quite the same. Less satisfactory substitutes are ground dried habanero chile and commercial habanero hot sauces. Other chile varieties can be used in place of habaneros, but why bother?

Every warning you've ever heard about handling chile peppers goes double for habaneros. First, when handling habaneros, use gloves to prevent your hands from burning and from transferring the capsaicin (the burning compound) to sensitive organs, such as the eyes. If one of your eyes ever burns when processing chiles, immediately flush it with a commercial eyewash. You will experience pain and the condition will seem more serious than it really is, but your eye will return to normal in about an hour.

Beware that the cutting board you use will retain some capsaicin, which can then be absorbed other foods, so scrub and rinse it well after cutting habaneros on it. Chile lore holds that household bleach can neutralize the capsaicin on cutting boards and knives. After puréeing habaneros in a blender do not sniff the mixture or you may be overwhelmed by the capsaicin-loaded fumes. When pulverizing dried habaneros in a spice mill, wear a painter's mask to minimize inhalation of the airborne powder. The mask will not prevent some sneezing, however, so sneeze away from the powdered habanero!

And what should you do if you overdose on habaneros and your mouth and tongue are on fire? We've tried every cure imaginable, from lemon juice to herbal teas, but the best cool-downs are dairy products—the thicker the better. Highly recommended are sour cream, yogurt, and milk.

As for beverages to serve with the habanero-based dishes: In the non-alcoholic category, we recommend fruit juices and punches—fresh limeade is great. The best alcoholic beverage is beer, which can handle heat levels that overwhelm wine. The carbonation seems to help with the heat, as well. A dairy-based dessert, such as an ice cream pie or a cheesecake makes a cooling finish to a habanero-infused meal.

So, break out the habaneros, pick a recipe, and prepare yourself for a culinary roller coaster ride!

Freshly harvested habaneros.

Elemental Concoctions: Salsas and Sauces

One of the most common uses for all chile peppers is in hot sauces and salsas, and habaneros are no exception. Since the habanero relatives are found in profusion throughout the Caribbean and the tropical Western Hemisphere, they are used in a variety of commercial products as well as in creative sauces (which are cooked) and salsas (which are not) prepared by home cooks. We have included a sampling from around the islands, the Yucatán, and South America.

The recipes range from simple sauces, such as Johnny's Food Haven Pepper Sauce, which combines habaneros with onions, garlic, and cilantro, to more complex blends with vegetables added for flavor and to adjust the heat level. Some are cooked, such as Haitian Hot Sauce, while some, such as Pebre from Latin America, are not. Due to their fruity aroma and flavor, habaneros and their relatives combine well with fruits, and with tropical fruits in particular. For example, our West Indies Pepper Sauce uses papaya and raisins as a base, and the herbs, vinegar, and mustard assist in producing a mixture of hot, sweet, and tart flavors.

Habaneros also lend themselves to other unusual sauces, such as our Hot Banana-Mango Ketchup and Habanero-Cilantro Mayonnaise, which will add a fiery kick to any sandwich. Two other interesting salsalike concoctions are Pineapple-Datil Marmalade and Spicy Mango-Tamarind Chutney. Remember, too, sauces and salsas are a great way to use up excess habaneros from the garden!

Johnny's Food Haven Pepper Sauce

The motto at Johnny's Food Haven in Port of Spain, Trinidad, is HOME COOKING AWAY FROM HOME, and this is one of Johnny's best home recipes. The aromatic herb that is traditionally used in this sauce is shadow bennie, or culantro, but since it is unavailable outside of the islands, we use cilantro. As a variation, you can add ½ to 1 cup of cooked and puréed pumpkin or carrots to make the sauce milder. Serve this sauce as an accompaniment to grilled meats, poultry, or fish.

> **5 Congo peppers or as many as can be stuffed into**
> **1 cup, seeds and stems removed**
>
> **1 cup water**
>
> **½ teaspoon salt**
>
> **1 onion, minced**
>
> **2 cloves garlic, minced**
>
> **¼ cup chopped fresh cilantro**

Place the chile peppers and water in a blender or food processor and purée until smooth. Transfer to a bowl and add all the remaining ingredients, stirring well. Let the mixture sit for at least 1 hour to blend the flavors.

Yield: About 2 cups
♥ EXTREMELY HOT

Belizean Habanero Hot Sauce

In order to preserve the habanero's distinctive flavor, we don't cook the chiles with the other vegetables, but instead add them afterward. To cut the heat of this very hot sauce, increase the amount of carrot or decrease the number of chiles. This sauce will keep for months in the refrigerator. Use this sauce for cooking as well as a table condiment. It goes particularly well with seafood dishes.

> **1 small onion, chopped**
>
> **2 cloves garlic, chopped**
>
> **1 tablespoon vegetable oil**
>
> **1 cup chopped carrots**
>
> **2 cups water**

> **3 to 4 habaneros, seeds and stems removed, minced**
> **3 tablespoons fresh lime juice**
> **2 tablespoons white vinegar**
> **I teaspoon salt**

In a skillet, sauté the onion and garlic in the oil until soft. Add the carrot and water and bring to a boil. Reduce the heat and simmer until the carrots are soft.

Remove from the heat and transfer to a blender or food processor. Add the chiles, lime juice, vinegar, and salt and purée until smooth. Serve at room temperature or chilled.

Yield: I½ cups
EXTREMELY HOT

Island Sherry Sauce

This recipe is reminiscent of Pickapeppa, a well-known Jamaican product. The longer the sauce steeps, the hotter it will become. Use this sauce in cooking or sprinkled over meats, poultry, or fish. It is also good as a marinade for grilled foods. *NOTE: This sauce must be made at least a week before serving.*

> **2 Scotch bonnets, seeds and stems removed, minced**
> **½ cup dry sherry**
> **¼ cup ketchup**
> **3 tablespoons soy sauce**
> **2 tablespoons fresh lime juice**
> **I tablespoon Tamarind Sauce (see Glossary)**
> **I tablespoon brown sugar**
> **I½ teaspoons dry hot mustard**

Combine all the ingredients in a bowl or jar, mix well, and let steep for 7 to 10 days to blend the flavors. The sauce will keep for months covered in the refrigerator.

Yield: I½ cups

West Indies Pepper Sauce

When you first taste this wonderfully fruity sauce, it gives the impression that it is going to be too hot to eat. But the searing heat never comes. Use it in cooking as well as a table condiment, glaze, or marinade.

3 Scotch bonnets, seeds and stems removed, chopped
2 cups white vinegar
I cup chopped onion
I can (15 ounces) diced papaya, including the juice
½ cup golden raisins
¼ cup malt vinegar
2 cloves garlic, minced
2 tablespoons fresh lime juice
I tablespoon chopped fresh ginger
2 tablespoons coriander
I teaspoon Dijon-style mustard
I teaspoon dried oregano
½ teaspoon ground turmeric

In a saucepan, combine all the ingredients and bring to a boil. Reduce the heat and simmer for 10 minutes. Transfer to a blender or food processor and purée until smooth. Allow the sauce to sit for at least 2 hours to blend the flavors. The sauce will keep for months covered in the refrigerator.

Yield: 2½ cups

Congo pepper, Trinidad.

Trinidad Rum Sauce

This sauce is definitely worth waiting the week it needs to steep. Use it to provide firepower for soups and stews, as well as fish, poultry, and meats. NOTE: This recipe must be made a week in advance.

> I cup light rum
> ½ cup chopped onion
> 5 Congo peppers, seeds and stems removed, coarsely
>   chopped

Combine all the ingredients in a bowl or jar and mix well. Let steep for 1 week, either in the refrigerator or at room temperature. Strain the sauce before using. The sauce will keep for months covered in the refrigerator.

Yield: I cup
❦ EXTREMELY HOT

Haitian Hot Sauce

Habanero-based hot sauces appear in many guises throughout the Caribbean and the Yucatán Peninsula. These sauces are flavorful as well as incendiary and this one is no exception. Use this sauce to add heat to cooked dishes, as a grilling sauce, or on the table as a condiment. NOTE: This recipe requires a couple of days' advance preparation.

> I onion, chopped
> 2 cloves garlic, chopped
> I tablespoon vegetable oil
> I tomato, chopped
> I½ cups white vinegar
> 6 piment bouc chiles, seeds and stems removed, chopped

In a skillet, sauté the onion and garlic in the oil until soft. Add the tomato and vinegar and simmer until all the tomatoes are soft.

Transfer the onion mixture to a blender or food processor and add the chiles. Purée until smooth. Put the mixture in a covered container and allow to steep for a couple of days in the refrigerator before serving.

Yield: 2 cups
❦ EXTREMELY HOT

Pebre

This hot sauce from Chile is typical of other Latin American sauces, such as the Argentine *chimichurri* and certain Colombian sauces. The characteristic that unites them is the use of a lot of greens—either parsley or cilantro—for flavoring. Pebre is great with grilled meats and barbecues.

2 habaneros, seeds and stems removed, coarsely
    chopped
3 tablespoons olive oil
juice of 3 lemons
1 tablespoon red wine vinegar
½ cup water
½ teaspoon salt
freshly ground black pepper, to taste
1 small purple onion, minced
2 cloves garlic, minced
½ cup finely chopped fresh parsley or cilantro

Place the chiles in a blender or a mortar and blend or grind to a paste. In a bowl, whisk together the oil, lemon juice, vinegar, water, salt, and pepper. Stir in the remaining ingredients and allow to sit at room temperature for at least 2 hours to blend the flavors before serving. Pebre will keep for a few days in the refrigerator.

Yield: 1 cup

Roasted Yucatecan Sauce

For this simple, all-purpose sauce, the vegetables are roasted before they are combined. This is characteristic of Yucatecan cuisine and imparts a distinctive roasted flavor. Don't worry about removing all the skins from the habaneros and tomatoes, as they will contribute additional flavor to the sauce. This sauce is wonderful over tacos, enchiladas, chiles rellenos, and tamales.

2 habaneros
4 tomatoes
1 small onion, unpeeled
¼ teaspoon oregano, Mexican preferred
2 tablespoons vegetable oil
¼ teaspoon salt

To roast the vegetables, place a large, dry skillet over high heat until very hot. Place the chiles, tomatoes, and onion in the skillet and roast, turning frequently, for 10 to 15 minutes. (If you have a stove-top grill, roast the vegetables over the flame until the skins are blackened, about 5 minutes. The vegetables can be roasted in a broiler as well.) Remove the vegetables from the skillet and, when cool enough to handle, peel off the skins with your fingertips or a knife. Chop the vegetables coarsely.

Place the chopped vegetables and oregano in a blender or food processor and purée until smooth.

In a skillet, heat the oil. Add the purée and sauté, stirring, about 5 minutes. Stir in the salt. This sauce will keep for 1 week the refrigerator.

Yield: About 2 cups

Hot Tomato Run Down Sauce

In Jamaica, this sauce is served over a wide variety of fish and even lobster, but it is so tasty that it's even wonderful tossed with pasta. The term *run down* (*oil down* in Barbados and Trinidad) refers to cooking vegetables in coconut milk until most of the milk is absorbed, so that only a light coating of oil remains.

> **2 cups coconut milk**
> **I onion, chopped**
> **3 cloves garlic**
> **4 tomatoes, peeled, seeded, and chopped**
> **2 Scotch bonnets, seeds and stems removed, chopped**
> **6 whole allspice berries**
> **I tablespoon chopped fresh thyme**
> **I tablespoon malt vinegar**
> **¼ teaspoon ground white pepper**
> **2 cups water**

In a saucepan, bring the coconut milk to a boil. Reduce the heat and add the onion and garlic. Simmer, uncovered, until the vegetables are soft. Add all the remaining ingredients and continue to simmer uncovered, until the sauce thickens and is reduced by half, about 30 minutes.

Place the sauce in a blender or food processor and purée until smooth. Strain the sauce before serving. This sauce is served hot. It will keep for about 2 days in the refrigerator.

Yield: 2 to 3 cups

Salpicón

The combination of habaneros and radishes in Yucatán was surprising to us when we first visited there. The radishes add both flavor and an interesting texture to this salsa. Bitter, or Seville, oranges are difficult to find outside of Yucatán, so we have provided a way to duplicate their flavor. As a variation to this recipe, you can add ¼ cup diced tomato or avocados. Serve this salsa as an accompaniment to seafood, chicken, and pork dishes.

> 2 habaneros, seeds and stems removed, minced
> I large purple onion, diced
> 8 to 10 radishes, trimmed and thickly sliced
> 3 tablespoons bitter orange juice* or fresh lime juice
> 3 tablespoons chopped fresh cilantro

Combine all the ingredients, except the cilantro, in a bowl and mix well. Allow to sit for 1 hour to blend the flavors. Add the cilantro, toss well, and serve.

Yield: I cup

Pineapple-Habanero Salsa

Here, hot habaneros are combined with sweet pineapple to make a condiment that goes well with almost any meat or poultry. The colors of this salsa make it an attractive garnish to nearly any plate.

> 2 cups chopped fresh pineapple
> 3 fresh tomatillos, husks removed and finely chopped
> I tablespoon fresh lime juice
> I tablespoon rice vinegar
> I tablespoon vegetable oil
> 2 teaspoons grated fresh ginger
> I teaspoon ground dried habanero
> 2 teaspoons chopped fresh mint

---

* Bitter orange juice: Combine ½ cup grapefruit juice, ¼ cup orange juice, and 3 tablespoons lime juice.

Combine all the ingredients in a bowl and mix well. Allow to sit for a couple of hours before serving. This salsa is best when served on the day it is prepared, but will keep for a couple of days in the refrigerator.

Yield: 2½ cups

Tropical Fruit Salsa

Other combinations of fruits will also taste great in this colorful salsa. Try adding diced melon, such as cantaloupe, honeydew, or musk. Diced mango is delicious, too, or, for a truly tropical and exotic salsa, add sliced star fruit. Tropical Fruit Salsa is a spicy and colorful accompaniment to fish or poultry.

> **½ cup diced fresh papaya**
> **½ cup sliced banana**
> **½ cup diced fresh pineapple**
> **¼ cup diced kiwifruit**
> **¼ cup diced red, green, or yellow bell pepper**
> **¼ cup diced purple onion**
> **1 Scotch bonnet, seeds and stem removed, minced**
> **2 tablespoons fresh orange juice**
> **1 tablespoon fresh lime juice**
> **2 tablespoons olive oil**
> **2 tablespoons pomegranate seeds**
> **2 tablespoons minced fresh cilantro**

Combine the papaya, banana, pineapple, kiwifruit, bell pepper, onion, and chile in a large bowl. In a small bowl, mix together the orange and lime juices and oil. Drizzle over the fruits and then toss gently to mix well. Allow to sit for 2 hours.

Just before serving, add the pomegranate seeds and toss well. Garnish with the cilantro.

Yield: 3 cups

Xnipec

The name of this salsa, which is pronounced *schnee-peck*, means dog's snout and undoubtedly refers to the fact that it is so hot it can make your nose run. Xnipec salsa frequently appears on dining tables in Yucatán and is best if eaten the day it is prepared.

2 habaneros, seeds and stems removed, chopped
2 tomatoes, chopped
I purple onion, chopped
⅓ cup fresh lime juice
3 tablespoons chopped fresh cilantro

Combine the chiles, tomatoes, onion, and lime juice in a bowl and mix well. Allow to sit for a couple of hours to blend the flavors. Just before serving, stir in the cilantro.

Yield: 2 cups

Dry Jerk Rub Seasoning

Dry jerk seasoning can be rubbed into meats or poultry for grilling, used as an ingredient in marinades and pastes, or as an addition to rice and vegetables. It is also good sprinkled on cooked foods instead of salt.

I teaspoon ground dried habanero
2 tablespoons onion powder
I tablespoon ground allspice
I tablespoon ground thyme
2 teaspoons ground cinnamon
2 teaspoons ground cloves
I teaspoon ground black pepper
I teaspoon garlic powder
½ teaspoon ground nutmeg

Combine all the ingredients in a bowl and mix well.

Yield: About ⅓ cup

Hellish Relish

This relish provides a nice crunchy texture that complements just about anything that is grilled. For a slightly different texture, grate rather than slice the vegetables.

> **2 habaneros, seeds and stems removed, minced**
> **I small jicama, peeled and cut into matchsticks**
> **2 carrots, peeled and cut into matchsticks**
> **I small cucumber, peeled and cut into matchsticks**
> **I small Granny Smith apple, or other tart green apple, peeled and cut into matchsticks**
> **6 green onions, including the tender green tops, thinly sliced on the diagonal**
> **¼ cup chopped purple onion**
> **½ cup pineapple juice**
> **2 tablespoons fresh lime juice**
> **¼ teaspoon ground cumin**
> **2 tablespoons chopped fresh parsley**

Combine all the ingredients except the parsley in a bowl and mix well. Allow to sit for a couple of hours to blend the flavors. Just before serving, stir in the parsley.

Yield: 4 cups

Texas habaneros.

Jerk Marinade

The technique of soaking foods in a liquid to flavor—or, in the case of meats, also to tenderize—was probably brought to the Caribbean by the Spanish. A marinade is perhaps easier to use than a paste, because it is thinner and coats better, and if you are grilling your jerk meats, the marinade can also be used as a basting sauce.

> 4 Scotch bonnets, seeds and stems removed, diced
> ¼ cup finely chopped onion
> 6 green onions, white part only, chopped
> ¼ cup red wine vinegar
> ⅓ cup vegetable oil
> 2 tablespoons soy sauce
> 2 tablespoons dark rum
> 1 tablespoon brown sugar
> 1 tablespoon minced fresh thyme
> 1 teaspoon freshly ground black pepper
> ½ teaspoon ground cloves
> ½ teaspoon ground nutmeg
> ½ teaspoon ground allspice
> ¼ teaspoon ground cinnamon

Combine all the ingredients in a bowl and mix well. Let sit for 1 hour to blend the flavors.

Yield: 1½ to 2 cups
EXTREMELY HOT

Hot Banana-Mango Ketchup

Although the base of the ketchup is commonly tomatoes, this one calls for tropical fruits. It will keep covered for up to a week in the refrigerator, or can be bottled for future use. The ketchup is wonderful spooned over grilled seafood.

½ cup finely diced onion
I tablespoon grated fresh ginger
2 cloves garlic, minced
2 tablespoons vegetable oil
4 canned mangoes, diced, plus I cup of the juice
3 ripe bananas, sliced
2 habaneros, seeds and stems removed
¼ teaspoon ground cloves
¼ teaspoon ground nutmeg
¼ teaspoon ground allspice
2 tablespoons brown sugar
¼ cup white vinegar
2 tablespoons chopped fresh basil
juice of I lime
salt, to taste

In a skillet, sauté the onion, ginger, and garlic in the oil until soft. Add all the remaining ingredients, except the lime juice and salt. Cover and simmer over a low heat, stirring frequently, for 20 minutes. Remove from the heat and purée in a blender or food processor until smooth.

Stir in the lime juice and salt. The ketchup should be a little thinner than you desire, as it will thicken as it cools. Use chilled or at room temperature.

Yield: 4 cups

Colombo Curry Paste

This fiery hot curry blend from Martinique is named after Colombo, the capital of Sri Lanka, which is appropriate as it reflects both the heat levels of the curries and the immigration of indentured laborers to Martinique from the Indian subcontinent. A curry paste gives more control over the heat than a powder.

1½ tablespoons coriander seeds
1½ tablespoons yellow mustard seeds
1½ tablespoons whole black peppercorns
1½ tablespoons cumin seeds
1½ teaspoons ground turmeric
3 cloves garlic, minced
1 tablespoon grated fresh ginger
3 habaneros, seeds and stems removed, minced

Place the coriander seeds, mustard seeds, peppercorns, cumin seeds, and turmeric in a blender or spice mill and grind to a coarse powder. Transfer to a mortar.

Add the garlic, ginger, and chiles, to the ground spices and mix well. Then, grind further in the mortar until a paste forms. Let sit for 1 hour at room temperature to blend the flavors.

Yield: ¼ cup
❧ EXTREMELY HOT

Datil peppers.

Pawpaw Pepper Mustard

Papayas, which are also called pawpaws in the West Indies, are tropical fruits with gelatinous black seeds. Here, they are used to make a mustard that is a welcome spicy, fruity change from the usual yellow mustard. Use it in place of regular mustard in any recipe, or on grilled meats, fish, or even grilled-cheese sandwiches.

> **2 tablespoons hot dry mustard powder**
> **¼ cup hot water**
> **3 habaneros, seeds and stems removed, chopped**
> **I ripe papaya, peeled, seeded, and chopped**
> **I cup diced onion**
> **¼ cup golden raisins**
> **¼ cup malt vinegar**
> **2 cloves garlic, minced**
> **2 tablespoons brown sugar**
> **I tablespoon rum**
> **¼ teaspoon ground turmeric**
> **I teaspoon salt**

In a cup, stir the dry mustard into the hot water until dissolved. Let sit for 5 minutes.

Combine the mustard mixture and all the remaining ingredients in a saucepan. Bring to a simmer over low heat and simmer, stirring frequently, until all the fruits are soft and the mixture has thickened, about 30 minutes. Remove from the heat and let cool. Place in a blender or food processor and purée until smooth. This mustard will keep for weeks in the refrigerator.

Yield: 2 cups
EXTREMELY HOT

Habanero-Cilantro Mayonnaise

This is an all-purpose spread. If thinned with milk, it makes a great salad dressing. It is delicious as a dip for raw vegetable sticks or spread on bread in place of plain mayonnaise.

> 1 cup coarsely chopped fresh cilantro
> ¼ cup water
> 1 tablespoon fresh lime juice
> 1½ tablespoons chopped garlic
> 2 habaneros, seeds and stems removed, chopped
> 2 cups mayonnaise
> ½ teaspoon salt

Place the cilantro, water, lime juice, garlic, and chiles in a blender or food processor and purée until smooth. Add to the mayonnaise in a bowl along with the salt and mix well.

Yield: 2½ cups
 EXTREMELY HOT

Peach-Habanero Chutney

The word *chutney* comes from the Sanskrit *chatni,* and in India refers to relishes that are used to accent other dishes. They can be sweet, sour, hot, or mild. This is a hot-and-sweet version. For a smoother chutney, purée in a blender or food processor before ladling into jars. Serve with poultry, fish, pork, or curries. This version is even good on toast or bagels.

> 1 teaspoon dried crushed habaneros
> 2 pounds peaches, peeled, pitted, and diced
> 2 cups white vinegar
> 1¼ cups light brown sugar
> ¼ cup fresh lemon juice
> 1 onion, minced
> ½ cup raisins
> 2 teaspoons yellow mustard seeds
> 1 teaspoon grated fresh ginger
> 1 teaspoon ground cinnamon
> ¼ teaspoon ground allspice

In a saucepan, combine all the ingredients and bring to a boil. Reduce the heat and simmer uncovered, stirring occasionally, until the sauce is thick, 45 minutes to 1 hour. Skim off any foam that forms. Let cool, transfer to jars, cover tightly and refrigerate for up to 2 weeks.

Yield: 3 cups

Spicy Mango-Tamarind Chutney

Chutneys will keep for a couple of weeks under refrigeration and are also suitable for canning. This chutney goes well with any curry dish.

> 1 pound ripe mangoes, peeled, pitted, and diced
> 2 tablespoons grated fresh ginger
> ¼ cup chopped onion
> 2 cloves garlic, minced
> 2 tablespoons Tamarind Sauce (see Glossary)
> 1 habanero, stem and seeds removed, chopped
> 1 cup golden raisins
> 1 cup sugar
> 2 cups malt vinegar
> ¼ teaspoon salt

In a saucepan, combine all the ingredients and bring to a boil. Reduce the heat and simmer, uncovered, until the mixture thickens, almost 15 minutes. Skim off any foam.

Let cool, transfer to jars, cover tightly, and refrigerate, for up to 2 weeks.

Yield: 2 to 3 cups

Pineapple-Datil Marmalade

This interesting sweet-sour jelly recipe was handed down within the Shugart family of St. Augustine, Florida. It was first published in *Chile Pepper* magazine.

> 2 datil peppers, seeds and stems removed
> 2 cups cranberry juice
> 1 can (16 ounces) crushed pineapple with juice
> 1 tablespoon fresh lemon juice
> 2 packages commercial pectin
> 3 cups sugar

Place the chiles, cranberry juice, pineapple and its juice, and lemon juice in a blender or food processor and purée until smooth.

Follow the directions for making jelly that come with the pectin.

Yield: 3 pints

Cleaning habaneros, Stonewall, Texas.

A Little Tingle Before the Feast: Eye-Opening Appetizers

This collection of appetizer recipes from a variety of places—and for varied tastes—delivers a hot introduction to any meal that is guaranteed to open the eyes of your guests. *Pastelles* are South America's version of tamales, and ours combine fruit, vegetables, beans, and pork with habaneros, all wrapped in banana leaves. Plantains provide another unusual wrapper; they encase shrimp and Scotch bonnets in the recipe for Plantain Pinwheels.

Shrimps regularly turn up in appetizers, and this chapter is no exception. While shrimp cocktails are common, our version from Yucatán serves the shellfish in a spicy broth instead of the usual thick tomatoey sauce. Deep-frying shrimps in a batter laced with coconut is popular in the Bahamas and other islands. Our recipe also adds some habanero hot sauce to the batter to offset the sweetness of the coconut. We even wrap shrimp and Scotch bonnets in phyllo pastry for a stunning and delectable appetizer, Fiery Ginger-Almond Shrimp in Phyllo Bundles.

Among other unusual seafood appetizers are the crisp Islands Conch Fritters and Habanero-Dusted Calamari Rings with Ginger Sauce. And, of course, we have included our favorite version of ceviche, which brings together swordfish, tropical fruits, coconut, and habaneros for an interesting twist on a venerable hot-and-spicy favorite.

Pastelles

These tasty snacks arrived in the Caribbean islands by way of South America, where banana leaves are used as wrappers. The leaves are available, frozen, in Asian markets. To soften them for use, thaw and then pass them over a gas flame, or place in a bowl and pour boiling water over them.

Filling:

½ pound ground pork
I large onion, minced
I clove garlic, crushed
I habanero, seeds and stem removed, minced
I cup diced, peeled yam
I cup cooked and drained black beans
I teaspoon minced thyme
I tablespoon red wine vinegar
I teaspoon minced basil
2 tomatoes, peeled and chopped
¼ cup drained capers, chopped
¼ cup raisins
¾ cup beef broth

Dough:

3 cups coarse cornmeal
2 tablespoons vegetable shortening
2 tablespoons vegetable oil
2 teaspoons salt
2¾ cups boiling water

3 or 4 banana leaves, cut into eighteen 8-by-10-inch
    rectangles
Johnny's Food Haven Pepper Sauce (page 42) or
    Haitian Hot Sauce (page 45)

To make the filling, sauté the pork in skillet until browned, breaking it up as it cooks. Add the onion, garlic, and chile and sauté for an additional couple of minutes. Add all the remaining filling ingredients and bring to a boil. Reduce the heat and simmer uncovered, for 45 minutes. Remove from the heat and cool.

To make the dough, place the cornmeal in a bowl and, using a pastry blender, cut in the shortening until crumbly. Stir in the oil and salt, and then pour in the boiling water, mixing well to form a smooth dough. Divide the dough into 18 equal portions and form each portion into a ball.

Place a ball of the dough in the center of a banana-leaf rectangle and press it out to form a ¼-inch-thick round. Spread about 2 tablespoons of the filling in the center. Fold half of the leaf over, bringing the cornmeal with it, and flatten into a rectangle. Repeat with the other half of the rectangle so that the dough encloses the meat. Fold up the leaf rectangle to make a package and tie securely with kitchen string.

Bring a large pot of salted water to a rapid boil. Add the packets, reduce the heat, and simmer uncovered, for 1½ hours. Remove and drain.

Snip the strings and serve with Johnny's Food Haven Pepper Sauce or Haitian Hot Sauce.

Yield: 18 pastelles

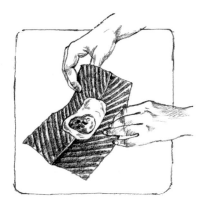

Plantain Pinwheels

The heat from the Scotch bonnet and the rum sauce complements the starchy sweetness of the plantains. Diced crab or lobster can be substituted for the shrimp in these appetizers.

> **4 ripe plantains**
> **6 medium shrimp, peeled, deveined, and finely minced**
> **2 tablespoons chopped green onions**
> **1 Scotch bonnet, seeds and stem removed, minced**
> **2 teaspoons Trinidad Rum Sauce (page 45)**
> **2 teaspoons chopped fresh basil**
> **1 teaspoon sesame oil**
> **1 teaspoon light soy sauce**
> **1 teaspoon cornstarch**
> **¼ teaspoon salt**
> **2 tablespoons, melted margarine or butter**

Preheat an oven to 325°F.

Peel the plantains and cut lengthwise into slices ⅛ inch thick. Cut off and discard the rounded ends.

In a bowl, combine all the remaining ingredients, except the butter, to form a paste. Spread the plantains with the shrimp paste. Roll up the slices into wheels and secure with toothpicks.

Place on an oiled baking pan and brush with the melted butter. Bake 15 minutes. Serve hot.

Yield: 12

Black Bean Dip with Toasted Pita Triangles

Black beans, sometimes known as turtle beans, are very popular in Latin America and throughout the Caribbean. This colorful dip not only looks good, but because the recipe substitutes baked pita for fried chips, is also good for you.

> **2 cups cooked and drained black beans**
> **¼ cup chopped purple onion**
> **¼ cup chopped red pepper**
> **¼ cup chopped orange segments**
> **2 tablespoons orange juice**
> **3 tablespoons balsamic or red wine vinegar**
> **2 cloves garlic, minced**
> **2 habaneros, seeds and stems removed, minced**
> **2 tablespoons chopped fresh cilantro**
> **8 large rounds pita bread**
> **3 tablespoons margarine, melted**
> **salt, to taste**

In a bowl, stir together the beans, onions, bell pepper, orange segments and juice, vinegar, garlic, chiles, and cilantro. Allow to sit for 1 hour to blend the flavors.

Preheat an oven to 375°F.

Cut the pita breads in half and then cut each half into triangles. Separate the triangle layers and then arrange the triangles, rough side up, on a baking pan. Brush with the margarine and season lightly with salt. Bake until crisp 10 to 12 minutes. Let cool before serving.

Serve the dip with the pita triangles.

Yield: 2½ cups

Curried Chicken Bites with Cool Cucumber Dip

We have served these "hot" appetizers with a cool accompaniment, but the Hot Banana-Mango Ketchup (page 53) or any of the hot sauces in this book will complement the chicken, too.

I pound skinless, boneless chicken, cut into small pieces
¼ cup minced onion
I large clove garlic
I egg, beaten
½ cup finely ground dried bread crumbs
2 teaspoons curry powder
I teaspoon ground ginger
½ teaspoon salt
½ teaspoon ground dried habanero
¼ teaspoon ground coriander
¼ teaspoon ground cloves
all-purpose four, for dredging
vegetable oil, for deep-frying
Cucumber Dip (recipe follows)

Place half of the chicken in a food processor and pulse until coarsely chopped. Transfer to a bowl. Repeat with the remaining chicken and add it to the bowl. Then add the onion, garlic, and egg to the chicken and mix well.

In another bowl, stir together the bread crumbs, curry powder, ginger, salt, ground habanero, coriander, and cloves. Add to the chicken and mix until well combined. Cover and refrigerate for 1 hour.

Shape the chicken mixture into 1-inch balls.

Pour the oil into a deep skillet into a deep skillet or a saucepan to the depth of 2 inches and heat to 370°F. Roll the chicken in the flour and shake off any excess. Fry the chicken balls for 5 minutes or until done, stirring occasionally. Remove and drain. Keep warm until all the balls are cooked.

Arrange the hot chicken balls on a platter and serve the dip alongside.

Yield: About 40 balls

CUCUMBER DIP

I cup (8 ounces) plain yogurt
½ cup grated unpeeled cucumber
I teaspoon fresh lemon juice
I teaspoon dried dill

In a bowl, combine all of the ingredients and mix well. Let sit for 1 hour at room temperature to blend the flavors.

Yield: About 1¼ cups

Spicy Olives

What could be more decadent than sitting on a verandah, sipping a gin and tonic, and snacking on these olives while gazing at the clear Caribbean sea? If you're lacking the sea, you can still enjoy these tasty olives and dream.

2 cups drained Kalamata olives
¼ cup olive oil
3 tablespoons red wine vinegar
I tablespoon chopped fresh rosemary
2 teaspoons minced habanero
3 cloves garlic, sliced
2 teaspoons lemon zest

Prick each olive several times with the point of a knife. Combine the olives with all the remaining ingredients in a bowl and mix well. Let sit at room temperature for at least 2 hours before serving.

Yield: 2 cups

Caribbean Coconut Shrimp with Hot Dipping Sauces

The sweetness of the coconut enhances the flavor of the shrimps. We like to serve these with a hot-and-sweet citrus dipping sauce, such as Pawpaw Pepper Mustard and Habanero-Orange Sauce.

> **3 tablespoons Belizean Habanero Hot Sauce (page 42)**
> **2 eggs, lightly beaten**
> **½ cup beer, allowed to go flat**
> **I cup sweetened, shredded coconut**
> **1½ cups all-purpose flour, plus extra for dredging**
> **vegetable oil, for deep-frying**
> **I pound medium shrimp, peeled and deveined**
> **Pawpaw Pepper Mustard (page 55)**
> **Habanero-Orange Sauce (recipe follows)**

In a bowl, whisk together the Belizean hot sauce, beer, the 1½ cups flour, and coconut. Allow to sit for 20 minutes.

Meanwhile, pour oil into a deep skillet of a saucepan to a depth of 3 inches and heat to 370°F. Dredge the shrimp in the flour, shaking off any excess. Dip the shrimp in the batter and then deep-fry until golden. Remove and drain.

Arrange the shrimp on a platter and serve the mustard and hot sauce on the side.

Yield: 20 to 24 shrimp

HABANERO-ORANGE SAUCE

> **½ cup orange marmalade**
> **¼ cup fresh orange juice, or to taste**
> **2 tablespoons white vinegar, or to taste**
> **¼ teaspoon hot dry mustard**
> **¼ teaspoon ground dried habanero**

Combine all the ingredients in a bowl and mix well. Thin with additional orange juice, or vinegar for a tarter sauce.

Yield: ¾ cup

Salbutes

These fried, puffed tortillas are common throughout the Yucatán Peninsula. Although usually served as an appetizer, we enjoyed ours in Belize as a lunch entrée sprinkled with liberal doses of habanero hot sauce. These are probably the most common fast food found in the region.

Tortillas:

  2 cups *masa harina*
  ¼ cup all-purpose flour
  ½ teaspoon baking powder
  1 teaspoon salt
  about ¾ cup water
  vegetable oil, for frying

Topping:

  2 chicken breast halves, poached, skin and bones
      removed, and meat shredded
  1 small onion, thinly sliced
  shredded cabbage
  Belizean Habanero Hot Sauce (page 42), for sprinkling

Stir together the *masa harina*, flour, baking powder, and salt in a bowl. Stir in enough of the water to make a stiff dough. Let the dough sit for 5 minutes.

Pinch off pieces of the dough and roll to make 1-inch balls. Then flatten each ball on a floured board with the palm of your hand into a round about 4 inches in diameter. Cook on a hot griddle until lightly done. Fry the tortillas in hot oil until crisp. Drain.

Top the tortillas with the chicken, onion, and cabbage. Sprinkle with the hot sauce and serve.

Yield: 12

Annotto Bay Pancakes

This scrumptious snack was cooked for us by Jack Shapansky, executive chef of the Ciboney Ocho Rios resort in Jamaica. (Annotto Bay is near Ocho Rios.) The pancakes can be served with Habanero-Orange Sauce (page 66).

I cup diced red bell pepper
2 onions, minced
6 small green onions, minced
¼ cup fresh thyme
4 cloves garlic, minced
2 Scotch bonnets, seeds and stems removed, minced
2 tablespoons butter or margarine
1½ pounds cooked lobster meat, diced
2 cups mayonnaise
1½ pounds sweet lobster meat, diced
2 cups mayonnaise
1½ pounds sweet potatoes, peeled, cooked, and coarsely mashed
3 egg yolks, lightly beaten
I teaspoon ground allspice
vegetable oil, for frying

In a skillet, sauté the bell pepper, onions, thyme, garlic, and chiles in the butter for 10 minutes. Remove from the heat.

Place half of the lobster and all of the mayonnaise in a blender or food processor and purée until smooth. Transfer the purée to a bowl and stir in the remaining lobster, the sautéed mixture, sweet potatoes, egg yolks, and allspice. Mix well and form into patties.

In a large skillet over medium-high heat, warm the oil. Slip the patties into the skillet, turning once or twice, until golden brown. Remove and drain on paper towels.

Yield: 20

Campeche Shrimp Cocktail

Serve this cocktail the way they do in Campeche, Mexico, in tall parfait glasses with the minced onion, cilantro, and habaneros served separately. That way diners can add just as much or as little as they want.

> 2 large tomatoes, roasted, peeled, seeds removed, chopped
>
> ¼ cup fresh orange juice
>
> 2 tablespoons fresh lime juice
>
> 2 tablespoons olive oil
>
> I teaspoon sugar
>
> ½ cup minced purple onion
>
> salt and freshly ground black pepper, to taste
>
> I pound shrimp, cooked, peeled, and deveined
>
> ¼ cup minced fresh cilantro
>
> 2 habaneros, seeds and stems removed, minced

In a skillet, place the tomatoes, orange and lime juices, and oil in a blender or food processor and purée until smooth. Transfer the purée to a saucepan and stir in the sugar and ¼ cup of the onion. Season with salt and pepper. Bring to a simmer and simmer for 10 minutes.

Divide the shrimps among 4 to 6 parfait glasses. Spoon the tomato mixture into the glasses to cover the shrimps. Place the remaining onion, cilantro, and habaneros in a mound on a plate and serve on the side.

Yield: 4 to 6 servings

California habaneros.

Tropical Chicken Kebabs

Spicy and sweet are two taste sensations that meld together well, as they do in these kebabs. The kebabs can also be served as a main dish over rice. If using bamboo skewers, soak in water for 20 minutes to prevent them from burning on the grill. NOTE: *This recipe requires advance preparation.*

2 Scotch bonnets, seeds and stems removed, minced
⅓ cup honey
½ cup cider vinegar
1 tablespoon soy sauce
1 tablespoon undiluted frozen orange juice concentrate
2 teaspoons orange zest
¾ teaspoon hot dry mustard
¾ teaspoon grated fresh ginger
2 boneless chicken breasts, cut into 1-inch cubes
banana slices
pineapple chunks
papaya chunks

Combine the chiles, honey, vinegar, soy sauce, orange juice, orange zest, mustard, and ginger in a saucepan. Bring to a simmer and simmer for 10 minutes. Remove from the heat and let cool to room temperature. Add the chicken, toss to coat well, cover, and marinate overnight in the refrigerator.

Preheat a broiler or prepare a fire in a charcoal grill. Thread the chicken and fruit on skewers. Broil 3 to 4 inches from the flame or grill over charcoal until done, basting frequently with the marinade, until the chicken is cooked through, about 15 minutes

Arrange on a platter and serve at once.

Yield: 4 servings

Out Islands Conch Fritters

Conch is popular throughout the Caribbean, and we couldn't get enough of these fritters when we were in the Bahamas. Unfortunately, conch can also be tough and chewy if it is not pounded with a mallet to tenderize it.

1 pound conch meat, pounded to tenderize
1 small onion, minced
1 celery stalk, minced
¼ cup minced green bell pepper
1 goat pepper, seeds and stem removed, minced
1 tablespoon fresh lemon juice
1 teaspoon minced fresh thyme
1 teaspoon minced fresh parsley
2½ all-purpose flour
2 teaspoons baking powder
about 1 cup water
vegetable oil for deep-frying

Finely chop the conch either by hand or in a food processor. Place it in a bowl and add the onion, celery, bell pepper, chile, lemon juice, thyme, and parsley and mix well.

Sift together the flour and baking powder into a bowl, and then stir the flour mixture into the conch mixture. Slowly add just enough water to make a stiff batter.

Pour oil into a deep skillet or saucepan to a depth of 3 inches and heat to 370°F. When the oil is hot, drop the batter by tablespoonful into the oil; do not crowd the pan. Deep fry until crispy and golden, 3 to 5 minutes. Using a slotted spoon, remove to paper towels to drain. Keep warm.

Arrange the hot fritters on a platter and serve with a hot sauce.

Yield: 6 servings

Habanero-Dusted Calamari Rings with Ginger Sauce

This calamari dish can be served as an appetizer or on a bed of greens as a terrific luncheon salad. If fresh squid is not available, substitute frozen.

> 1 pound squid, cleaned and cut into rings (tentacles are not used)
>
> ground dried habanero
>
> ¼ cup peanut oil
>
> 2 teaspoons sesame oil
>
> 2 tablespoons grated fresh ginger
>
> 3 small green onions, including the green tops, finely chopped
>
> 2 teaspoons soy sauce
>
> juice of 2 limes, plus lime wedges for garnish

Lightly dust the squid with the ground habanero. Heat the oils in a skillet and sauté the calamari until opaque, about 1 minute. Remove and keep warm.

Add the ginger, green onions, soy sauce, and lime juice to the skillet and sauté until the onions are soft, about 2 minutes. Return the squid to the pan and toss with the sauce.

Place on a platter and garnish with lime wedges. Serve immediately.

Yield: 4 servings

Gulf Stream Swordfish Ceviche

Fish "cooked" in juice is popular wherever there are fresh seafood and hot chiles. This ceviche is a variation on the more typical mixture of fish, onion, and chiles. NOTE: *This recipe requires advance preparation.*

> ½ pound swordfish fillets, cut into ½-inch cubes
>
> ½ pound whole small scallops
>
> ¾ cup fresh orange juice, plus extra orange juice for serving
>
> ¼ cup fresh lime juice
>
> 1 habanero, seeds and stem removed, minced
>
> 1 cup diced papaya
>
> 3 tablespoons grated coconut, lightly toasted

Combine the fish, scallops, orange and lime juices, and habanero in a nonreactive bowl and toss to mix. Cover and refrigerate, turning occasionally, until the fish loses its translucency and turns opaque, about 4 hours.

Just before serving, drain the fish. Return it to the bowl and add the pineapple, papaya, and remaining orange juice to moisten. Divide equally among 6 to 8 parfait glasses and garnish with the coconut.

Yield: 6 to 8 servings

Salmon-Habanero Pâté

Serve this pate as a spread with crusty bread or crackers and garnished with hard-cooked egg wedges, tomatoes, and olives.

> 1 habanero, seeds and stem removed, minced
> 2 tablespoons Dijon-style mustard
> ½ pound cooked salmon, either canned or fillets
> 3 tablespoons light rum
> 2 hard-cooked eggs, coarsely chopped
> 3 tablespoons minced onion
> 2 tablespoons fresh lemon juice
> ¼ cup sour cream
> salt, to taste

Place all the ingredients in a blender or food processor and purée until smooth. Transfer to a bowl and refrigerate for 1 hour before serving.

Yield: 1½ cups

Round pepper, Trinidad.

Fiery Ginger-Almond Shrimp in Phyllo Bundles

The trick to working with phyllo pastry is to keep it from drying out. Always thaw frozen phyllo in the refrigerator. Once it is at room temperature, keep the sheets you are not working with covered with a slightly damp cloth. These shrimp bundles take some work to make, but they can be prepared ahead of time and frozen. If they have been frozen, bake (unthawed) for an 2 additional minutes.

> ½ teaspoon grated fresh ginger
> 1 Scotch bonnet, seeds and stem removed, minced
> ½ cup plus 1 tablespoon butter or margarine
> 2 teaspoons almond liqueur, such as amaretto
> ¾ pound shrimp, peeled deveined, and coarsely chopped
> 3 tablespoons almonds, toasted
> 9 sheets phyllo dough, each about 16 by 12 inches
> 3 tablespoons finely ground dried bread crumbs

In a skillet, sauté the ginger and chile in 1 tablespoon butter for 2 minutes. Add the almond liqueur and the shrimp and continue to sauté until the shrimp just turns pink. Remove, let cool, and stir in the almonds.

Preheat an oven to 350°F.

To assemble the bundles, in a small pan melt the remaining ½ cup butter and immediately remove from the heat. Brush 1 sheet of phyllo with the butter and sprinkle ½ tablespoon of the bread crumbs evenly over it. Starting from a short end, fold it in half, so it looks like a book, with the bread crumbs inside. Brush the top with more butter. Now cut it in half lengthwise and then in thirds crosswise to make squares.

Place a teaspoonful of the filling in the center of each square. Gather up the corners of the square and gently twist the top to seal. Cover the bundles with a lightly dampened kitchen towel while preparing the remaining bundles.

Place the bundles on a baking sheet and brush the tops lightly with the remaining melted butter. Bake until golden brown, about 10 minutes. Let cool slightly before serving.

Yield: 36 appetizers

The Seemingly Innocent: Searing Soups and Sizzling Salads

Ah, they look so harmless, but boy are they potent. For spicy-food lovers who just can't get enough heat, we offer a group of soup and salad recipes certain to please. We have included variations on traditional soups as well as some truly hot innovations. From Spicy Sweet Soup, first served to us in Costa Rica, to an authentic Minorcan Clam Chowder from St. Augustine, the pungent flavor of the *chinense* clan holds forth.

And who said searing soups must be served hot? Our Island Gazpacho is a tropical variation of the old Spanish favorite, and chilled Pineapple-Mango Salsa Soup marries tropical fruits and incendiary habaneros.

The salads run the gamut from the venerable Mayan Xol-Chon Pico de Gallo to a hot twist on an old favorite—coleslaw. Our version, called Green Mango Slaw with Papaya Seed Dressing, slips in some ingredients your mother never imagined: mangoes, papayas, and habaneros. Other unusual salads include Goat Pepper Conch Salad, which is yet another way to serve the popular Caribbean mollusk, and tropical Hearts of Palm Jerk Salad, in which tender hearts of palm are combined with Jamaican seasonings.

Since habaneros and their relatives combine so well with fruits, we've also included Coconut-Watermelon Salad with Lime-Habanero Dressing and Chile Fruit Sundae. With their sweet heat, these two salads can double as desserts.

Spicy Sweet Potato Soup

Arlene Lutz, a well-known television cooking celebrity, served a version of this soup to us when we visited her restaurant in Escazú, Costa Rica. Arlene's secret is to add a little sugar if the potatoes are not sweet enough.

4 cups chicken broth
2 cups diced, peeled sweet potatoes
3 tablespoons fresh orange juice
¼ teaspoon orange zest
3 tablespoons heavy cream
½ teaspoon ground dried habanero
pinch of white pepper
chopped fresh cilantro, for garnish

Bring the broth to a boil in a saucepan. Add the sweet potatoes and boil until they are soft. Drain, reserving the broth in the saucepan.

Place the sweet potatoes and some of the broth in a blender and purée the mixture until smooth. Add the purée to the reserved broth, along with the orange juice and zest, cream, chile, and white pepper. Bring to a simmer and simmer for 20 minutes.

Garnish with cilantro.

Yield: 4 servings

Trinidad seasoning pepper.

Apricot-Carrot Soup

Habaneros are not unusual in soups, but the addition of fruit is. This soup is not delicious as a luncheon entrée served with rolls and a crisp garden salad.

> **2 teaspoons minced fresh ginger**
>
> **1 large shallot, chopped**
>
> **1 tablespoon butter or margarine**
>
> **2 habaneros, seeds and stems removed, minced**
>
> **2 cups diced carrots**
>
> **10 dried apricot halves, plus sliced dried apricots, for garnish**
>
> **4 cups chicken broth**
>
> **1 tablespoon fresh lime juice**
>
> **½ teaspoon ground nutmeg**
>
> **¼ cup evaporated milk**
>
> **¼ cup heavy cream**

In a saucepan, sauté the ginger and shallot in butter until soft, about 5 minutes. Add the chiles, carrots, apricots, and broth and bring to a boil. Reduce the heat and simmer until the carrots are tender, about 30 minutes.

Place the mixture in a blender and purée until smooth. Return the purée to the pan and reheat. Stir in the lime juice, nutmeg, milk, and cream. Simmer, stirring occasionally, until thickened, about 10 minutes.

Garnish with sliced apricots and serve.

Yield: 4 servings

Congo pepper.

Pepperpot Soup with Herb Dumplings

Pepperpots—which can refer to either a soup or a stew—are popular throughout the Caribbean, and this recipe is for the soup, not the stew. We have substituted easy-to-find ingredients for the more unusual items, such as spinach for callaloo and potatoes for taro. We have also added spices, herbs, and, of course, Scotch bonnets to the dumplings.

Soup:

- 1 pound beef shanks
- ½ pound salt pork, rind removed
- 1 large onion, chopped
- 4 green onions, including the green tops, chopped
- 2 cloves garlic, minced
- ½ teaspoon dried thyme
- 2 quarts water
- 1 bunch fresh spinach, trimmed and chopped
- 1 potato, peeled and diced
- 2 Scotch bonnets, seeds and stems removed, minced
- 6 small okra
- 2 tablespoons butter or margarine
- 1 cup coconut milk
- 1 cup cooked small shrimp, shelled and deveined
- salt and freshly ground black pepper, to taste

Habanero harvest.

Dumplings:

- ½ **cup cornmeal**
- ½ **cup all-purpose flour**
- **I teaspoon baking powder**
- **I½ teaspoons salt**
- **I teaspoon ground nutmeg**
- **3 tablespoons butter, chilled**
- **2 tablespoons chopped fresh parsley**
- **I Scotch bonnet, seeds and stem removed, minced**
- **2 to 4 tablespoons cold water**

To make the soup, place the beef shanks, salt pork, onion, green onions, garlic, and thyme in a pot and add the water. Bring to a boil and boil for 5 minutes, skimming off any foam that forms. Reduce the heat and simmer until the beef is tender, about 1 hour.

Remove the shanks and salt pork. Discard the salt pork. Cut the meat from the shanks and then, using two forks, shred the meat; set it aside. Add the spinach, potato, yam, and chiles to the pot. Cover and simmer for an additional 30 minutes.

Meanwhile, to make the dumplings sift together the cornmeal, flour, baking powder, salt, and nutmeg into a bowl. Add the butter and, using 2 forks or your fingers, cut in the butter. Add the parsley and chile and stir just enough of the water for the dumpling dough to hold together. Use 2 teaspoons to form and drop the dumplings into the simmering soup and stir to keep them from sticking together. Cover and simmer the dumplings for 15 minutes.

Meanwhile, in a skillet sauté the okra in the butter until lightly browned on all sides. Add them to the soup, re-cover, and simmer for 5 minutes.

Return the shredded meat to the pot. Stir in the coconut milk and shrimp. Add salt and pepper, heat through and serve.

Yield: 8 servings

Caribbean Black Bean Soup

Black beans are a staple throughout much of the Caribbean, as well as Mexico and Central America, and they are prepared in a variety of ways. This hearty soup can be puréed as described here or the beans can be left whole. Look for epazote (see Glossary) in Latin American markets. NOTE: *This recipe requires advance preparation.*

2 cups dried black beans
I cup beer
3 habaneros
I large onion, chopped
4 cloves garlic, minced
2 tablespoons vegetable oil
I large ham hock
I cup canned tomatoes, chopped, along with the juice
I tablespoon dried epazote, optional
2 teaspoons ground coriander
½ teaspoon ground cumin
¼ teaspoon ground cloves
I tablespoon red wine vinegar
6 to 8 cups water
2 tablespoons tequila, optional
sour cream and chopped fresh cilantro, for garnish

In a large bowl, combine the beans, beer, 1 whole chile, and water to cover. Let stand overnight.

The next day, remove and discard the chile from the beans. Remove the seeds and stems from the remaining habaneros and mince the chiles. In a skillet, sauté the minced chiles, onion, and garlic in the oil until soft, about 5 minutes.

Transfer the beans and their liquid to a pot. Add the sautéed chile mixture and all the remaining ingredients except the tequila and garnish. Bring to a boil, reduce the heat, and simmer, uncovered, until the beans are soft, 3 to 3½ hours. Add water as needed.

Remove the ham hock when cool enough to handle, cut the meat from the bones and shred; set aside.

Divide the soup in half and purée half in a blender until smooth. Return the purée to the soup remaining in the pot. Add the shredded ham and simmer the soup, uncovered, until thickened to desired consistency, about 15 minutes.

Remove from the heat, and stir in the tequila (if using). Ladle into bowls and garnish with the sour cream and cilantro and serve.

Yield: 6 to 8 servings

Island Gazpacho

What could be better than a cold, spicy soup on a hot tropical day? All you need is a warm sea breeze, turquoise blue water, and some crusty French bread to make a perfect meal in paradise.

> 1 slice white bread, crusts removed, cubed
> ½ cup water
> 2 large tomatoes, peeled, seeded and chopped
> 2 cups pineapple or guava juice
> 1 cup cubed pineapple, fresh preferred
> 1 cup cubed papaya, fresh preferred
> 1 red bell pepper, seeds and stem removed, diced
> 1 cucumber, peeled and coarsely chopped
> 4 green onions, chopped
> ¼ cup fresh lime juice
> 1 Scotch bonnet, seeds and stem removed
> 2 tablespoons olive oil
> crushed ice, for serving
> 2 tablespoons chopped fresh cilantro
> freshly ground black pepper, to taste

Place the bread in a bowl and add the water. When the bread has absorbed the water, squeeze out as much of the water as possible, and place the bread in a blender or food processor. Add all the remaining ingredients except the cilantro and black pepper and purée until smooth. (This step may need to be done in batches.)

Transfer the soup to a nonreactive bowl, cover and refrigerate for 2 hours.

To serve, ladle into bowls set over crushed ice. Garnish with the cilantro and freshly ground pepper.

Yield: 4 to 6 servings

Minorcan Clam Chowder

A consistent winner of the annual Great Chowder Debate in St. Augustine, Florida, this recipe is authentically Minorcan. It's delicious, too! The longer the chowder simmers, the more flavorful it will become.

> ½ pound salt pork
> 2 large onions, chopped
> I clove garlic, chopped
> I green bell pepper, seeds, ribs, and stem removed, chopped
> I can (12 ounces) whole tomatoes, with juices
> I teaspoon dried thyme
> I quart shelled fresh clams, cooked and chopped, with liquid
> 2 cups hot water
> salt and freshly ground black pepper, to taste
> I datil pepper, seeds and stem removed, halved

In a saucepan, sauté the salt pork until the fat is rendered. Remove the salt pork, dice, and set aside.

Add the onions, garlic, and bell pepper to the pan and sauté until the onions are lightly browned. Stir in the tomatoes and their juices and the thyme and bring to a boil. Once the mixture is boiling, break up the tomatoes with a spoon. Reduce the heat and simmer, uncovered, until the mixture is thick, about 1 hour.

Add the diced meat, the clams and their liquid, and the hot water. Cover and simmer until the clams are cooked. Don't overcook, as they will become tough. Season with salt and pepper, add the chile, and simmer for 5 minutes before serving. Ladle into bowls and serve at once.

Yield: 6 servings

Chicken-Chile Soup

Here's a superhot variation on old-fashioned chicken soup. The amount of capsaicin in this recipe is sure to cure any cold! For a leaner soup, chill it in the freezer until the fat congeals on top and then lift off and discard.

Spiced Stock:

- 1 fryer chicken, about 3 pounds, cut into pieces
- 2 carrots, peeled and chopped
- 2 habaneros, seeds and stems removed, minced
- 1 large onion, chopped
- 1 celery stalk, coarsely chopped
- ½ red bell pepper, seeds, ribs, and stem removed, chopped
- 1 tomato, chopped
- 1 teaspoon salt
- 1 teaspoon sugar
- 1 teaspoon whole black peppercorns

Soup:

- 4 cups spiced stock
- 2 green onions, thinly sliced
- 1 red bell pepper, seeds, ribs and stems removed, thinly sliced
- 2 tablespoons dry sherry or Island Sherry Sauce (page 43)
- 2 cups shredded chicken, from making the stock
- chopped fresh thyme or parsley, for garnish

To make the stock, combine all the ingredients in a large saucepan and add water to cover. Bring to a boil and boil, uncovered, for 10 minutes, skimming off any foam that rises to the surface. Reduce the heat, cover, and simmer until the chicken begins to fall off the bones, about 50 minutes. Allow the chicken to cool in the stock.

Remove the chicken from the stock and discard the skin and bones. Using 2 forks, shred the meat and set aside. (You should have about 2 cups.) Measure the stock and, if needed, add water. Strain the stock to equal 4 cups.

To make the soup, place the stock in a saucepan and bring to a simmer. Add the green onions, bell pepper, and sherry. Simmer, uncovered, for 5 minutes.

To serve, divide the shredded chicken evenly among 6 to 8 bowls. Ladle the soup into the bowls and garnish with the herbs.

Yield: 6 to 8 servings

Pineapple-Mango Salsa Soup

Here's another cold yet hot soup. It has a pleasantly fiery bite and a wonderfully fruity taste.

2 cups pineapple chunks, fresh preferred

1 cucumber, peeled, seeded, and chopped

2 green onions, chopped

1 teaspoon finely chopped Scotch bonnet

1 cup chopped mango

1 yellow bell pepper, seeds, ribs, and stem removed, finely chopped

1 cup unsweetened pineapple juice

¼ cup fresh lime juice

2 tablespoons chopped fresh cilantro

1 teaspoon sugar

salt, to taste

Place the pineapple, cucumber, green onions, and chile in a blender or food processor and purée until smooth.

Transfer the purée to a bowl and add all the remaining ingredients. Stir to mix well.

Cover and refrigerate for 1 hour before serving.

Yield: 4 to 6 servings

Unamed *chinense*.

Coconut-Watermelon Salad with Lime-Habanero Dressing

This is a simple, cool, and refreshing salad that is great served along-side jerk dishes or other barbecues. Bananas, cantaloupe, and oranges or other tropical fruits can be added or substituted to change the taste and texture of this salad.

Lime-Habanero Dressing:
¼ cup fresh lime juice
2 teaspoons sugar
1 teaspoon minced habanero
salt, to taste

Salad:
1 cucumber, unpeeled, seeded, and diced
1 cup diced watermelon
¼ cup shredded coconut, lightly toasted, for garnish
chopped fresh mint, for garnish

To make the dressing, combine all the ingredients in a salad bowl and stir well. Allow to sit at room temperature for 1 hour to blend the flavors.

To make the salad, combine the cucumber and watermelon, add the dressing, and toss until thoroughly coated. Sprinkle the coconut and mint over the top and serve.

Yield: 2 to 4 servings

Hearts of Palm Jerk Salad

Hearts of palm are literally the heart of the tender shoots of the palm trees that are found throughout the Caribbean and Brazil. The tough outer husks are removed and the insides are then boiled until tender. Hearts of palm are almost impossible to find fresh outside of the islands and Central America, but they can be found canned in many stores.

> 1 teaspoon **Dry Jerk Rub Seasoning (page 50)**
> 2 tablespoons **vegetable oil**
> **juice of 1 lime**
> **shredded lettuce**
> 1 **can (15 ounces) hearts of palm, drained and sliced**
> 1 **large tomato, sliced**
> **chopped green onions**
> **pimento-stuffed green olives, sliced**

Whisk the jerk seasoning, oil, and lime juice together in a bowl.

Arrange the hearts of palm and tomato slices on the lettuce. Sprinkle the onions over the top and then drizzle on the dressing. Scatter on the olives, and serve.

Yield: 4 servings

Pimenta do cheiro, **Brazil.**

Chile Fruit Sundae

The combination of fresh fruit and chile is quite common in Mexico, where you can purchase fresh fruits dusted with ground chile from vendor carts on street corners. The blending here of hot and sweet provides a refreshing beginning or end to any meal.

> **3 tablespoons cider vinegar**
> **2 tablespoons sugar**
> **¼ teaspoon dried crushed habanero**
> **I cup cubed watermelon**
> **I cup cubed fresh pineapple**
> **I cup sliced fresh strawberries**

In a saucepan, combine the vinegar and sugar and heat, stirring until the sugar dissolves. Stir in the chile and let cool

Place the fruits in a bowl and pour the cooled vinegar mixture over the top. Cover and chill until serving.

Yield: 4 servings

Xol-Chon Pico de Gallo

This recipe from Yucatán is more of a salad than a salsa, even though it is called *pico de gallo*, a name associated with salsas. A nice accompaniment to grilled meats, it could even be served as a chilled fruit dessert.

> **2 oranges, peeled and sectioned**
> **I small jicama, peeled and diced**
> **3 tablespoons fresh lime juice**
> **I tablespoon fresh orange juice**
> **I habanero, seeds and stem removed, minced**
> **2 tablespoons chopped fresh cilantro**

Chop the oranges in roughly the same size pieces as the jicama and combine in a bowl.

Mix the lime juice, orange juice, and chile in another bowl and then pour it over the jicama mixture. Toss well. Let stand at room temperature for 1 hour to blend the flavors.

Toss the salad with the cilantro and serve.

Yield: 4 servings

Goat Pepper Conch Salad

This recipe is based on a salad from the Ivory Coast Restaurant on Paradise Island in the Bahamas, where *chinenses* are called goat peppers. Abalone can be used in place of the conch; prepare it the same way.

1 pound conch meat, pounded until tender and chopped
2 goat peppers, seeds and stems removed, minced
1 large onion, finely chopped
2 celery stalks, finely chopped
1 red or green bell pepper, seeds, ribs, and stem removed, finely chopped
2 tomatoes, chopped
¼ cup finely chopped pimento
juice of 4 limes
3 tablespoons olive oil
salt, to taste
shredded lettuce

Combine all the ingredients except the lettuce. Toss to mix well and let stand for a couple of hours to blend the flavors. The lime juice will "cook" the conch meat.

Serve on a bed of shredded lettuce.

Yield: 6 servings

Costa Rican habaneros.

Green Mango Slaw with Papaya Seed Dressing

Here is a tropical change from the usual celery-seed coleslaw. Allow the dressing to sit as long as possible to build up the heat. Store extra dressing in the refrigerator and use on tossed greens or fresh fruit salad.

Salad:

- 2 green mangoes, peeled and pitted
- ½ papaya, peeled
- I cup finely shredded cabbage
- I small purple onion, thinly sliced

Dressing:

- ½ papaya, peeled and chopped, reserving 3 tablespoons of the seeds
- 2 tablespoons sugar
- ¼ cup cider vinegar
- I habanero, seeds and stem removed, chopped
- ½ cup vegetable oil
- salt and freshly ground black pepper, to taste

chopped fresh watercress, for garnish

To make the salad, cut the mangoes and papaya into thin strips ¼ inch wide and 2 inches long. Combine the mangoes, papaya, cabbage, and onion in a salad bowl.

To make the dressing, place the papaya and papaya seeds, sugar, vinegar, and chile in a blender. With the motor running, slowly add the oil. Continue to blend until the mixture is puréed and the seeds look like ground pepper. Season with salt and pepper. Let sit for at least 2 hours.

To serve, drizzle just enough of the dressing over the salad to coat lightly, and then toss gently. Garnish with the watercress.

Yield: 4 to 6 serving
♦ EXTREMELY HOT

Crab and Cantaloupe Salad with Habanero Yogurt

We have used our habanero-spiked yogurt dressing on a crab salad here, but it would taste equally good on shrimp. In fact, this dressing goes well on even a simple salad of tossed garden greens. Although the yogurt cuts the heat of the habaneros, you might still want to use only one of them in this dressing.

Dressing:

- 1 cup plain yogurt
- ¾ cup chopped cucumber
- ½ cup mayonnaise
- 3 tablespoons chopped fresh cilantro
- 2 cloves garlic, minced
- 2 habaneros, seeds and stems removed, minced
- 2 tablespoons fresh lime juice
- 2 tablespoons vegetable oil
- ¼ teaspoon sugar
- pinch of white pepper

Salad:

- 1 pound cooked crab meat
- 1 small cantaloupe, diced
- 1 avocado, diced
- 1 small purple onion, thinly sliced and separated into rings

To make the dressing, combine all the ingredients in a blender or food processor and purée until smooth. Transfer to a bowl and allow to sit at room temperature for 1 hour to blend flavors.

Toss the crab, cantaloupe, and avocado with the dressing. Top with the onion rings and serve.

Yield: 4 to 6 servings

Buljol

The name of this shredded salt fish dish comes from the French *brule*, meaning "burnt," and *geule*, which is slang for "mouth" and refers to the burning sensation from the chile. Although this is a salad, it is traditionally served in Trinidad for breakfast or Sunday brunch. If salt cod is unavailable, use cooked and flaked white fish fillets in its place.

½ pound boneless, salt cod
1 large onion, minced
1 large tomato, chopped
1 yellow wax chile, seeds and stem removed, minced
1 Congo pepper, seeds and stem removed, minced
freshly ground black pepper, to taste
3 tablespoons olive oil
lettuce leaves, whole or shredded
sliced hard-cooked eggs and avocado, for garnish

Place the salt cod in a bowl and pour boiling water over it to cover. Allow it to sit for 1 hour, pour off the water, then repeat with more boiling water, again allowing it to sit for 1 hour. Drain the cod, remove and discard any skin or bones, squeeze out all the water, and shred the fish.

In a bowl, combine the fish, onion, tomato, yellow and Congo peppers, black pepper, and olive oil. Toss to mix well.

Place the mixture on the lettuce. Garnish with the eggs and avocado and serve.

Yield: 4 servings

Tossed Garden Salad
with Champagne-Habanero Vinaigrette

This is a hot and tasty variation of the usual vinaigrette that gains heat the longer it sits. Any combination of greens will do, as the dressing turns even an ordinary green salad into something special.

Vinaigrette:
- 2 cloves garlic, minced
- 1 Scotch bonnet, seeds and stem removed, minced
- ¼ cup Champagne vinegar or white wine vinegar
- 1 tablespoon fresh orange juice
- ½ cup olive oil
- 2 teaspoons Dijon-style mustard
- ¾ teaspoon sugar
- ¼ teaspoon ground cumin
- freshly ground black pepper

Salad:
- mixed salad greens, such as radicchio, butter crunch, arugula, and red-leaf lettuce
- sliced cucumber
- grated carrot
- sliced radishes
- black olives, for garnish

To make the vinaigrette, whisk together in a small bowl or combine in a jar, cover and shake well. Allow to sit for 1 hour to blend the flavors. To make the salad, combine all the ingredients and drizzle on the dressing. Toss to mix, garnish with the olives, and serve.

Yield: ¼ cup dressing

Do the Jerk:
Of Goats, Pigs, Chickens, and
the Occasional Steer

Habanero lovers are always inventing interesting ways to cook with their favorite chiles. Michael Bordes, who lives in The Colony, Texas, recommends placing an unpunctured whole habanero or Scotch bonnet on top of a chicken or a piece of meat that is to be roasted. During cooking, the meat is gradually infused with the fruity flavor of the chile and only a touch of heat.

Probably the one dish most closely associated with Caribbean cooking is jerk pork. We have provided a basic jerk paste that can be used with a pork roast, as well as with pork chops or chicken. Another Caribbean favorite is curry goat, which is extremely popular in Jamaica and Trinidad. We have modified the recipe slightly with the addition of apricots and raisins. Incidentally, the power of the habaneros can be illustrated with just one example: When Tim McGann of Houston's Calypso restaurant makes curry goat, he uses just one ounce of chopped habaneros for every thirty pounds of meat!

This chapter also explores the pairing of habaneros and fruits. The potent chiles are married with cherries in Marinated Grilled Pork Chops with Habanero Cherry Sauce, with oranges in Scotch-Bonneted Pork Chops, with mangoes in Roast Lamb with Tropical Caribe Sauce, and with lemons in Citrus Cashew Chicken.

Jerk Pork

No collection of Scotch bonnet recipes would be complete without one for this Jamaican classic. We have substituted an oven for the traditional barbecue pit used for cooking this dish. Thick pork chops will work as well as a roast in this recipe and, once marinated, can be baked, broiled, or grilled. The jerk seasoning is also good on chicken. NOTE: *This recipe requires advance preparation.*

> **1 pork roast, 3 to 4 pounds**
> **Jerk Paste (recipe follows)**

Place the roast in a shallow nonreactive container and rub the paste over the entire surface. Cover and marinate in the refrigerator overnight.

Bring the roast to room temperature. Preheat an oven to 400°F.

Place the roast on a rack in a roasting pan. Place in the oven and immediately reduce the heat to 325°F. Roast for 1½ hours, or until a meat thermometer inserted into the thickest portion registers 150°F.

Yield: 6 to 8 servings

JERK PASTE

> **3 Scotch bonnets, seeds and stems removed, chopped**
> **½ cup chopped green onion**
> **2 tablespoons red wine vinegar**
> **3 tablespoons vegetable oil**
> **1 tablespoon soy sauce**
> **1 tablespoon fresh lime juice**
> **½ cup Tamarind Sauce (see Glossary)**
> **2 tablespoons crushed pimiento berries**
>   **(or 1 tablespoon ground allspice)**
> **2 teaspoons grated fresh ginger**
> **1 teaspoon ground cinnamon**
> **¼ teaspoon ground nutmeg**

Combine all the ingredients in a blender or food processor and purée until smooth. This paste will keep covered in the refrigerator for up to 3 weeks.

Yield: 1 cup
EXTREMELY HOT

Scotch-Bonneted Pork Chops

The complex mix of fruit and herb flavors in the coating goes well with such accompaniments as scalloped or baked potatoes and asparagus spears or green beans NOTE: *The chops must marinate for at least a couple of hours before cooking.*

½ cup pineapple juice, fresh preferred
¼ cup fresh orange juice
3 tablespoons fresh lime juice
¼ cup chopped onion
1 Scotch bonnet, seeds and stem removed, chopped
1 tablespoon chopped fresh cilantro
2 teaspoons orange zest
6 tablespoons vegetable oil
4 pork loin chops

Place all the ingredients except the chops and 2 tablespoons of the oil in a blender or food processor and purée until a loose paste is formed. Place the chops in a nonreactive dish and coat them on both sides with the paste. Cover and marinate in the refrigerator for 2 to 3 hours.

Pour the remaining 2 tablespoons of oil into a skillet. Add and pan-fry, turning once and coating with additional paste, until done.

Yield: 4 servings

Bolivian red *chinense*.

Marinated Grilled Pork Chops with Habanero-Cherry Sauce

This recipe is from Chimayo restaurant in Pontiac, Michigan. It was sent to *Chile Pepper* magazine by executive chef Brian Polcyn and chef-de-cuisine Steve Phillips. They feature a number of hot-and-spicy recipes, but this is one of their signature chile dishes. NOTE: *This recipe requires advance preparation.*

¼ cup brown sugar
¼ cup Dijon-style mustard
2 tablespoons soy sauce
6 pork loin chops
1 carrot, finely chopped
1 celery stalk, finely chopped
½ onion, finely chopped
1 tablespoon grated fresh ginger
2 fresh thyme sprigs
1 tablespoon minced shallot
1 bay leaf
3 whole black peppercorns
6 tablespoons butter
¾ cup port wine
1 pound fresh cherries, stemmed and pitted
1 habanero, seeds and stem removed, minced
3 cups pork or chicken broth
2 tablespoons cornstarch mixed with 1 tablespoon water
salt and freshly ground black pepper, to taste

In a small bowl, mix together the sugar, mustard, and soy sauce. Place the chops in a nonreactive dish and spread the mixture evenly over both sides. Cover and marinate in the refrigerator for 4 to 5 hours.

In a skillet, sauté the carrot, celery, onion, ginger, thyme, shallot, bay leaf, and peppercorns in 2 tablespoons of the butter until the onion turns golden brown. Add the wine, raise the heat, and simmer until thickened, about 20 to 30 minutes.

Add the cherries and habanero and cook until all the juices are released from the cherries. Stir in the broth and bring to a boil. Reduce the heat and simmer for 45 minutes. Strain the sauce through a very fine sieve into a saucepan, pressing with a spoon to extract all the juices.

Heat the sauce over a low heat. Whisk the remaining 4 tablespoons of butter into the sauce, 2 tablespoons at a time. Raise the heat and stir in the cornstarch mixture. Continue to cook, stirring until the sauce thickens enough to coat the back of a spoon, about 5 to 10 minutes.

Grill the pork chops to desired doneness and serve with the sauce ladled over them.

Yield: 6 servings

Braised Pork in Tangy Tamarind Sauce

Tamarind, that sour legume, is often combined with *chinense* varieties around the Caribbean. Bottled tamarind sauce can be substituted for the homemade sauce called for here. Look for it, as well as the tamarind paste, in Asian stores. Serve this pork dish with Spiced-Up Rice and Peas (page 135), vegetables, and fruit salad.

> I tablespoon soy sauce
> I clove garlic, minced
> I habanero, seeds and stem removed, minced
> I pound boneless pork tenderloin, cut into I¼-inch cubes
> 3 tablespoons vegetable oil
> ¼ cup sherry or Island Sherry Sauce (page 43)
> ¼ cup Tamarind Sauce (see Glossary)
> I tablespoon white vinegar
> I cup pork or chicken broth
> I cup water
> I teaspoon cornstarch mixed with I tablespoon water

Combine the soy sauce, garlic, and chile in a nonreactive bowl. Add the pork to the sauce, and marinate at room temperature for 1 hour.

In a skillet, brown the pork in the oil. Remove the pork to a bowl and drain off the oil from the pan.

Pour the sherry into the skillet. Deglaze the pan, scraping up any browned bits. Add the Tamarind Sauce, vinegar, broth, and water, and bring to a boil. Reduce the heat to low and add the pork. Cover and cook at low heat until the meat is very tender, about 45 minutes. The liquid should be reduced by one-third.

Stir the cornstarch mixture into the sauce and simmer, stirring, to thicken.

Yield: 4 servings

Aztec Grilled Pork Kebabs

This recipe mixes pork and pineapple, but just about any combination of fruits and vegetables, such as papaya, onions, and tomatoes, will taste great. One teaspoon crushed or ground dried habanero chiles can be used if fresh chiles are unavailable. The kebabs are delicious on a bed of rice. If you use bamboo skewers, soak them in water for 20 minutes to prevent them from burning on the grill.

> 2 cups pineapple juice
> 1 small onion, chopped
> 2 habaneros, seeds and stems removed, chopped
> 1 teaspoon dried oregano
> 1 tablespoon fresh lime juice
> 1 teaspoon soy sauce
> ¼ teaspoon ground cinnamon
> 1 pound boneless pork tenderloin, cut into 1¼-inch cubes
> 1 cup pineapple wedges
> 1 red or green bell pepper, seeds, ribs, and stem
>   removed, cut into 1-inch squares
> 1 zucchini, cut into 1-inch pieces
> 2 teaspoons cornstarch mixed with 2 tablespoons water
> ¼ cup raisins
> vegetable oil

In a bowl, stir together the pineapple juice, onion, chiles, oregano, lime juice, soy sauce, and cinnamon. Place the pork in a nonreactive bowl, add half of the marinade, and toss to coat evenly. Cover and marinate in the refrigerator for 2 hours.

Prepare a fire in a charcoal grill.

Thread the pork cubes onto skewers alternately with the pineapple, bell pepper, and zucchini pieces.

In a saucepan, bring the remaining marinade to a boil. Reduce the heat and stir in the cornstarch mixture. Then stir in the raisins and simmer, until the sauce thickens. Keep warm.

Brush the skewered foods with oil and place the skewers on a grill rack. Grill, turning once, until the meat is done and the vegetables are still crisp, about 8 minutes.

To serve, drizzle the warm sauce over the meat and serve any additional sauce on the side.

Yield: 4 to 6 servings

Roast Lamb with Tropical Caribe Sauce

The creamy, hot fruit sauce complements the sometimes strong flavor of the lamb. The sauce can be used over pork, beef, or even chicken. Although this is not an authentic Caribbean dish, it will add a tropical island taste to any meal.

4 pounds boneless lamb shoulder
3 cloves garlic, crushed
1 tablespoon vegetable oil
1 tablespoon crushed black pepper

Sauce:
½ cup coconut milk
1 cup diced pineapple
3 tablespoons sugar
2 teaspoons grated fresh ginger
½ teaspoon ground allspice
2 habaneros, seeds and stems removed, minced
1 mango, peeled, pitted, and diced
1 banana, chopped
2 tablespoons fresh lime juice
¼ cup dry white wine

Place the lamb on a plate and rub it all over with the garlic. Brush with the oil and sprinkle the pepper over the top. Cover and let stand at room temperature for 1 hour.

Preheat an oven to 325°F.

Place the lamb on a rack in a roasting pan. Roast for 2 hours or until a meat thermometer inserted into the thickest part registers 150°F. Remove from the oven and keep warm.

To make the sauce, in a saucepan, combine the coconut milk, pineapple, sugar, ginger, allspice, and habaneros. Bring to a simmer and continue to simmer for 7 to 8 minutes. Remove from the heat and let cool for 5 minutes. Transfer to a bowl and add the mango, banana, lime juice, and wine. Stir well.

Thinly slice the meat, and arrange on individual plates. Spoon some of the sauce over the meat. Serve the remaining sauce in a bowl on the side.

Yield: 8 to 10 servings

Apricot Curry Goat

Curries were brought to the Caribbean by Indian immigrants and quickly became popular. Goat is used throughout the Caribbean, but lamb makes a good substitute. Serve this curry over plain white rice with a fruit chutney and topped with grated coconut.

> **2 pounds boneless goat meat, trimmed of excess fat and cut into 1½-inch cubes**
>
> **3 tablespoons vegetable oil**
>
> **1 onion, chopped**
>
> **1 tablespoon chopped garlic**
>
> **2 tablespoons Colombo Curry Paste (page 54)**
>
> **¼ teaspoon ground nutmeg**
>
> **1 tablespoon minced Scotch bonnets**
>
> **3 cups beef broth**
>
> **½ cup chopped dried apricots, plus some for garnish**
>
> **¼ cup golden raisins**
>
> **½ cup chopped canned plum tomatoes, with juice**
>
> **3 tablespoons apricot preserves**
>
> **¼ cup slivered blanched almonds**
>
> **1 cup coconut milk**
>
> **freshly ground black pepper, to taste**
>
> **2 tablespoons fresh lime juice**
>
> **3 cups cooked rice**
>
> **grated fresh coconut, for garnish**
>
> **Spicy Mango-Tamarind Chutney (page 57)**

In a large skillet, brown the goat meat on all sides in the oil. Remove and keep warm. Add the onion and garlic to the skillet and sauté until soft, about 5 minutes. Stir in the curry paste, nutmeg, and Scotch bonnet and simmer, stirring constantly, for 2 minutes.

Pour in 1 cup of the broth, raise the heat to high and deglaze the skillet, scraping up any browned bits. Return the lamb to the pan along with any juices that have collected on the plate. Add the dried apricots, raisins, tomatoes, apricot preserves, almonds, coconut milk, the remaining 2 cups broth, and the ground pepper and bring to a boil. Reduce the heat, cover, and simmer until the meat is very tender, about 1 hour.

Remove from the heat and stir in the lime juice. Serve over rice garnished with the grated coconut and chopped apricots. Serve the chutney on the side.

Yield: 6 servings

Bistec Ranchero

This quick, simple-to-prepare dish is a kind of south-of-the-border stir-fry. Traditional refried beans, Mexican rice, and warmed tortillas round out this hot and spicy dish from the Yucatán in Mexico.

> **2 large tomatoes, roasted, peeled, seeds removed, chopped**
>
> **I onion, cut into thin wedges and separated into layers**
>
> **2 cloves garlic, minced**
>
> **I habanero, seeds and stem removed, minced**
>
> **2 tablespoons olive oil**
>
> **I pound sirloin steak, cut into ¾-inch-wide strips**
>
> **¼ teaspoon ground cumin**
>
> **chopped fresh cilantro**
>
> **flour tortillas, warmed**

In a wok or deep skillet, sauté the onion, garlic, and chile in the oil until soft but still crisp. Add the beef and sauté until browned, about 7 minutes. Add the tomatoes and cumin and stir well, and simmer for 2 minutes

Garnish with the cilantro. Serve with warmed tortillas.

Yield: 4 to 6 servings

Wild Brazilian *chinense*.

Black Bean Picadillo

Picadillos are very popular throughout all of Latin America and there are many variations, including this one from Cuba. Almost any type of beans, such as kidney or pinto beans, can be used. You can turn this dish into a vegetarian main course by leaving out the meat.

> 1 pound lean beef, diced
> 2 tablespoons vegetable oil
> 1 large onion, chopped
> 4 cloves garlic, minced
> 5 *rocotillo* chiles, seeds and stems removed, minced
> 1 green bell pepper, seeds, ribs, and stem removed, chopped
> 1 teaspoon freshly ground black pepper
> ½ teaspoon ground cinnamon
> ½ teaspoon ground cloves
> ¼ teaspoon ground allspice
> ¼ teaspoon ground oregano
> 2 tomatoes, peeled and chopped
> 2 to 3 cups beef broth
> 2 tablespoons red wine vinegar
> ½ cup golden raisins
> 1 large tart apple, peeled, cored, and diced
> 1 can (16 ounces) black beans, drained and rinsed

In a dutch oven, brown the beef in the oil. Add the onion, garlic, chiles, bell pepper, black pepper, spices, and oregano and sauté for 2 minutes. Add the tomatoes, broth, vinegar, and raisins and simmer until the meat is very tender, 30 to 45 minutes. Add more broth if necessary.

Add the apple and beans and simmer for an additional 15 minutes.

Yield: 6 servings

Shredded Beef and Melongene in Habanero Hot Sauce

Melongene is the word for eggplant in Trinidad. The crispy shredded beef provides an interesting texture, at the same time and offsets the softness of the eggplant. Serve this dish on a bed of rice accompanied by citrus, carrots, and a tossed green salad.

> 1 pound tender beef, such as sirloin steak
>
> 1 small onion, chopped
>
> 4 cloves garlic, minced
>
> 2 habaneros, stems removed but pods left whole
>
> ¼ cup finely minced fresh chives
>
> 2 tablespoons grated fresh ginger
>
> 1 tablespoon soy sauce
>
> 1 tablespoon rum
>
> 1 tablespoons cornstarch
>
> 1 eggplant, peeled and cut into 1-inch cubes
>
> 3 tablespoons olive or vegetable oil
>
> 1 tablespoon habanero hot sauce, such as
>   Belizean Habanero Hot Sauce (page 42) or Haitian
>   Hot Sauce (page 45)
>
> 1 teaspoon sugar
>
> 1 cup beef broth
>
> 2 cups cooked white rice

Place the beef, onion, half of the garlic, and the chiles in a saucepan. Add water to cover. Bring to a boil, reduce the heat, cover, and simmer until the meat starts to fall apart, about 1 hour.

Remove from the heat and drain. Using 2 forks, shred the meat.

Combine the chives, ginger, soy sauce, rum, cornstarch, and the remaining garlic in a bowl. Add the meat, toss to mix, and allow to sit at room temperature for 1 hour.

In a large skillet, quickly fry the eggplant in the oil until browned. Pour off all but 1 tablespoon of oil from the skillet. Add the beef mixture to the same pan and sauté for 2 minutes.

Return the eggplant to the pan with the beef. Add the hot sauce, sugar, and broth, and simmer until the liquid is reduced by half, about 15 minutes. Serve with white rice.

Yield: 4 servings

Caribbean Chicken

This chicken dish tastes like it is more difficult to prepare than it actually is. By following the basic recipe and substituting different fruits and juices, such as papaya, mango, and guava juice, you can alter the fruity flavors.

½ cup chopped onion

I clove garlic, minced

I tablespoon vegetable oil, plus vegetable oil, for browning

2 Scotch bonnets, seeds and stems removed, minced

I cup fresh orange juice

½ cup fresh pineapple juice

I cup chicken broth

I tablespoon white vinegar

I tablespoon dark rum (optional)

I tablespoon sugar

I tablespoon orange zest

½ teaspoon ground cinnamon

½ teaspoon ground cloves

I fryer chicken, about 3 pounds, cut into serving pieces

all-purpose flour, for dredging

½ cup diced pineapple, fresh preferred

Preheat an oven to 350°F.

In a skillet, sauté the onion and garlic in the 1 tablespoon of oil until soft. Add the chiles, orange and pineapple juices, broth, vinegar, rum (if using), sugar, orange zest, cinnamon, and cloves. Stir well and simmer the sauce until slightly thickened, about 20 to 30 minutes. Remove from the heat.

Dredge the chicken pieces in the flour, then brown them well in a skillet, using vegetable oil. Transfer the chicken to a baking dish. Pour the sauce over the chicken and add the pineapple. Bake, uncovered, until the chicken is done, basting the chicken occasionally with the sauce, as it cooks. Serve with the sauce over the top, or serve the sauce in a bowl on the side.

Yield: 4 servings

Citrus Cashew Chicken

Any citrus fruit juice will work in this recipe. Try tangerine, orange, or even a combination, such as lemon and lime. Adding habaneros, with their fruity heat, complements the citrus flavor of the sauce.

⅓ cup rice wine or dry sherry

2 tablespoons light soy sauce

I egg white

2 tablespoons cornstarch

¼ teaspoon ground white pepper

I pound skinless and boneless chicken, cut into
    I-inch cubes

peanut oil for frying

2 tablespoons lemon zest

I tablespoon minced garlic

2 teaspoons minced fresh ginger

I habanero, seeds and stem removed, minced

3 tablespoons sugar

¼ cup fresh lemon juice

I cup chicken broth

I tablespoon cornstarch mixed with 2 tablespoons water

I cup roasted cashew nuts

Combine 1½ tablespoons of the wine, ½ tablespoon of the soy sauce, the egg white, and white pepper in a bowl and stir to mix. Add the chicken and toss to coat. Allow to sit for 10 minutes.

Combine 1 tablespoon of the lemon zest, the garlic, and chile in a small bowl. In another small bowl, stir together the sugar, lemon juice, and broth to make a sauce.

In a skillet, heat the oil to 350°F. Add the chicken and fry until lightly browned, 5 to 7 minutes. Remove and drain.

Pour off all but 1 tablespoon of the oil from the skillet. Add the garlic mixture and stir-fry for 10 seconds. Add the lemon juice mixture and bring to a boil. Slowly stir in just enough of the cornstarch mixture to thicken the sauce. Return the chicken to the sauce, add the cashews, and heat through.

Garnish with the remaining 1 tablespoon lemon zest. Serve immediately.

Yield: 4 servings

Yardie Chicken

Here is a classic fricasseed chicken from Montego Bay, Jamaica. The people who live in the shantytown area of Montego Bay call themselves yardies, hence the name of this down-home dish. And, in parts of the Caribbean chayote squash is called *cho-cho*.

1 red bell pepper, seeds, ribs, and stem removed, chopped

1 green bell pepper, seeds, ribs, and stem removed, chopped

1 large onion, chopped

8 green onions, including the green tops, chopped

2 carrots, peeled and sliced ¼ inch thick

¾ cup finely chopped celery tops

8 okra pods, sliced ½ inch thick

1 *cho-cho* (chayote squash), peeled and chopped

1 Scotch bonnet, seeds and stem removed, finely chopped

2 cloves garlic, minced

1½ tablespoons fresh thyme

3 chicken legs with thighs attached

1½ cups milk

all-purpose flour, for dredging

vegetable oil, for frying

2 jars (4 ounces) sliced pimentos, drained

In a bowl, combine the bell peppers, onion, carrots, celery, okra pods, *cho-cho*, chile, garlic, and thyme. Mix well. Place the chicken pieces in a nonreactive dish, cover with the vegetable mixture, and marinate for 2 hours.

Remove the chicken pieces, scraping off any vegetables. Reserve the vegetables. Pour the oil into a large pan to a depth of 1 inch and heat. Dip the chicken into the milk and then dredge in the flour, shaking off any excess. Reserve the remaining milk. Slip the chicken into the hot oil and pan-fry until golden brown, about 20 minutes. Transfer chicken to a plate. Drain off all but 1 tablespoon of the oil from the pan.

Reduce the heat and pour ½ cup of the milk into the pan. Deglaze the pan, scraping up any browned bits. Add the vegetable mixture and braise for a couple of minutes longer. Push the vegetables aside in several places and return the chicken pieces to the pan. Add enough of the reserved milk to reach halfway up the sides of the chicken.

Simmer for 25 minutes, stirring the vegetables occasionally and taking care not to knock the breading off the chicken. Turn the chicken pieces, add the pimientos, and continue to simmer, stirring occasionally, until the chicken is done, about 20 minutes.

If the gravy is too thick, thin with additional milk; if it is too thin, raise the heat and reduce until thickened. Spoon the hot gravy over chicken and serve.

Yield: 6 servings

Roast Bajan Chicken

Bajan blends are combinations of herbs and spices used to flavor both chicken and fish in Barbados. Use the bajan as a marinade, or make slits in the chicken and stuff it into the slits. Or do as we have done, and slip the mixture under the skin of the chicken before cooking.

> 2 bonney peppers, seeds and stems removed, chopped
> 6 green onions, including the green tops, chopped
> 3 cloves garlic, chopped
> 2 tablespoons chopped fresh parsley
> I tablespoon minced fresh garlic
> ½ teaspoon ground cloves
> ¼ teaspoon ground cumin
> I teaspoon freshly ground black pepper
> 2 tablespoons fresh lime juice
> 2 tablespoons vegetable oil, or as needed
> I roasting chicken, 3 to 4 pounds
> melted butter or margarine

Place all the ingredients, except the chicken and butter, in a blender or food processor. Purée to a paste, adding more oil if necessary.

Using your fingers, loosen the skin from the breast of the chicken, and spread the paste between the skin and the meat. Cover and let marinate in the refrigerator for a couple of hours.

Preheat an oven to 450°F. Place the chicken on a rack in a roasting pan. Brush with the melted butter, place in the oven, and immediately reduce the temperature to 350°F. Roast the chicken, basting occasionally with the pan juices, about 1½ hours. Remove from the oven and let sit for 5 minutes before carving.

Yield: 4 servings

Spiced-Up Chicken in Coconut Shells with Mango Cream

This dish is really worth the effort, because it is an elegant and delightfully tropical presentation. To test if a coconut is fresh, pound a nail into one of the "eyes," drain the coconut water, and taste. If it tastes sweet, it is fresh. To open the coconut, bake it at 375°F for 15 minutes, let cool, and then, using a hacksaw, cut it in half.

> 2 coconuts, drained, liquid reserved, and cut in half
>
> 2 cloves garlic, minced
>
> 1 tablespoon butter or margarine
>
> 1 tablespoon olive oil
>
> 1 pound skinless and boneless chicken, cut into
>   1-inch cubes
>
> 1 onion, minced
>
> 1 Scotch bonnet, seeds and stem removed, minced
>
> 1 tablespoon minced fresh ginger
>
> 1 tablespoon chopped fresh cilantro, plus extra
>   for garnish
>
> 2 teaspoons ground cardamom
>
> 2 teaspoons ground cinnamon
>
> 2 teaspoons Colombo Curry Paste (page 54)
>
> ¼ teaspoon ground cumin
>
> ¼ teaspoon ground cloves
>
> 1 tablespoon cornstarch
>
> ½ cup light cream
>
> 1 large ripe mango, peeled, pitted, and diced

Preheat a broiler.

Pry the coconut meat from the shells, leaving a ¼-inch-thick layer of meat attached to the shells. Reserve the shells. Cut 2 cups of the meat into thin slivers and grate 1 cup of the remaining meat . Spread the grated coconut in a pan and place under the broiler. Toast, shaking the pan frequently, until the coconut is golden brown, 5 to 10 minutes. Reserve to use for garnish.

In a large skillet, sauté the garlic in the butter and oil for 1 minute. Add the chicken and sauté until browned. Transfer the chicken to a bowl and keep warm. Add the onion, chile, ginger, and reserved coconut slivers. Sauté for an additional 5 minutes.

Stir in the reserved coconut water and 1 tablespoon cilantro and return the chicken to the pan. Add the cardamom, cinnamon, curry paste, cumin, and cloves and stir well. Cover and simmer for 30 minutes.

Stir together the cornstarch and cream and add to the chicken, along with the mango and cook until thickened, about 5 minutes. Spoon into the coconut shells. Garnish with the cilantro and toasted coconut and serve.

Yield: 4 servings

Chicken Breast with Macadamia Nut-Orange Sauce

In this recipe, pine nuts, almonds, or pistachios can be substituted for the macadamias. Accompany with rice pilaf made with chicken broth.

> **4 chicken breasts**
> **¼ cup vegetable oil**
> **½ cup chopped onion**
> **I tablespoon grated fresh ginger**
> **2 teaspoons minced garlic**
> **3 cups chicken broth**
> **½ cup chopped macadamia nuts, plus additional chopped and toasted, for garnish**
> **I habanero, stem removed but pod left whole**
> **½ teaspoon lemon zest**
> **½ teaspoon orange zest**
> **2 teaspoons brown sugar**
> **I teaspoon ground coriander**
> **⅛ teaspoon saffron threads**

In a skillet, brown the chicken in the oil. Remove chicken and keep warm. Pour off all but 1 tablespoon of the oil, add the onion, and sauté until browned. Add the ginger and sauté for 2 minutes. Add 1 cup of the broth and deglaze, scraping up any browned bits. Remove from the heat. Combine the remaining broth, nuts, chile, zests, brown sugar, coriander, and saffron in a blender and purée until smooth.

Pour the purée into the skillet, return the chicken to the pan, and bring to a boil. Reduce the heat, cover, and simmer until the chicken is tender and the sauce has thickened, about 30 minutes. To serve, transfer the chicken to a platter. Top with the sauce and garnish with macadamia nuts.

Yield: 4 servings

Xin-Xin Chicken

This Brazilian dish reflects the African influence on the cuisine in Bahia. Traditionally, this version of chicken in a shrimp-and-nut sauce would use *dende* (palm) oil to add color and flavor. But since the oil is difficult to find and is loaded with saturated fats, we have substituted paprika. The dried shrimp can be found in Latin and Asian markets.

I chicken, 3 to 4 pounds, cut into serving pieces
¼ cup fresh lemon juice
I onion finely chopped
3 cloves garlic, minced
¼ cup dried shrimp
2 *pimentas do cheiro*, seeds and stems removed, minced
2 teaspoons grated fresh ginger
2 to 3 tablespoons olive oil
½ teaspoon paprika
I large tomato, peeled, seeded, and coarsely chopped
I cup chicken broth
½ pound fresh shrimp, peeled and deveined
2 tablespoons ground cashew nuts
2 tablespoons chopped fresh parsley, for garnish

Place the chicken in a nonreactive dish and sprinkle the lemon juice over it. Turn the chicken to coat evenly, then cover and marinate for 30 minutes.

In a large skillet, sauté the onion, garlic, dried shrimps, chiles, and ginger in 2 tablespoons of the oil until the onion is soft. Add the chicken pieces and brown, adding the remaining oil if necessary, to prevent sticking. Reduce the heat, cover, and simmer until the chicken is cooked through when pierced with a knife, 30 to 45 minutes. Add the shrimp and ground cashews and raise the heat slightly. Simmer until the shrimp are cooked and the sauce is thickened, about 10 minutes.

Garnish with the parsley.

Yield: 4 to 6 servings

Diving the Blue Hole: Scallops to Spiny Lobster to Snapper

Because most of the regions that grow habaneros and their relatives adjoin the sea, the combination of seafood and the *chinense* clan is ubiquitous. Our selection of seafood reflects the versatility of these pungent pods. They're sealed in parchment in Pompano en Papillote, marinated in fruit-infused tequila in Grilled Salmon Borracho with Habanero-Lime Butter, paired with avocados in Charbroiled Halibut Steaks with Salsa de Aguacate, served with peaches and apricots in Braised Monkfish with Gingered Fruit Cream, and sweetened with honey in West Indies Pepper Shrimp.

At the Maya restaurant in St. Barthelemy in the Dutch West Indies, grilled fish is served with a key lime and the local version of the habanero. The stem end of the chile is cut off so that the pepper forms a small cup. Guests are instructed to squeeze the lime juice into the chile, swirl it around, and pour it over the fish. Try this simple method with the recipes in this chapter.

Pompano en Papillote

En papillote is French for preparing food in cooking parchment. Fish *en papillote* makes a highly dramatic presentation: The bags puff up as they cook and are all served on individual plates to be opened at the table. If parchment is unavailable, use brown paper cut from shopping bags.

> 3 shallots, chopped
>
> 3 *rocotillos* or 1 habanero, seeds and stems
>   removed, minced
>
> 2 tablespoons margarine
>
> 2 tablespoons all-purpose flour
>
> 2 cups milk
>
> 1 egg, lightly beaten
>
> 3 tablespoons dry white wine
>
> 2 tablespoons habanero hot sauce, such as
>   Belizean Habanero Hot Sauce (page 42) or
>   Haitian Hot Sauce (page 45)
>
> ¼ teaspoon grated nutmeg
>
> 1 cup cooked tiny shrimp
>
> 1 cup chopped cooked lobster or crab meat
>
> 4 pompano or other white fish steaks, about
>   ¼ pound each

Preheat an oven to 350°F.

In a skillet, sauté the shallots and chile(s) in the margarine until soft. Stir in the flour and cook, stirring, for 2 minutes.

Slowly add the milk and the egg, stirring constantly, and simmer until the sauce starts to thicken. Add the wine, hot sauce, and nutmeg, and simmer until the mixture thickens again. Remove from the heat and fold in the shrimp and crab.

Cut out 4 pieces of parchment each about 15 by 12 inches. Starting from a short side, fold each piece in half. Cut out each piece in the shape of a heart and open out flat. Place some of the sauce on one-half of each heart and top each with a fish steak. Spoon any remaining sauce over the fish.

Fold the uncovered half of each heart over the fish to cover completely and then crimp together the edges to seal securely. Place the packets on a greased baking sheet and bake until puffed, about 30 minutes.

Remove from the oven and serve immediately.

Yield: 4 servings

Grilled Salmon Borracho with Habanero-Lime Butter

The subtle flavor of this marinade doesn't overpower the wonderful taste of fresh salmon. Serve with Belizean Coconut Rice (page 136) and broccoli florets.

4 salmon steaks

Marinade:
¼ cup vegetable oil
½ cup fresh orange juice
3 tablespoons fresh lime juice
1 tablespoon tequila
1 tablespoon lime zest
1 tablespoon minced habanero
1 clove garlic, minced

Butter:
¼ cup butter, at room temperature
1 tablespoon fresh lime juice
2 teaspoons minced habanero
2 teaspoons lime zest
¼ teaspoon garlic salt

Place the salmon steaks in a single layer in a nonreactive dish. In a small bowl, stir together all the ingredients for the marinades. Pour over the salmon, coating evenly. Let marinate at room temperature, turning frequently, for 2 hours.

Meanwhile, to make the butter, in a bowl, beat the butter until smooth, then beat in all the remaining ingredients. Cover and refrigerate until 15 minutes before serving.

Prepare a fire in a charcoal grill. When the coals are ready, place the salmon steaks on the grill rack and grill, turning once and basting frequently with the marinade, until it flakes when pierced with a fork or until done as desired. Transfer the salmon to individual plates. Top with the butter and serve.

Yield: 4 servings

Crispy Fish with Caramelized Onion Relish

In the islands, this dish might be made with the popular flying fish, but since they don't fly very far from the Caribbean, you can substitute snapper or other white fish, such as bass, perch, flounder, or grouper. For a tamer version, omit the ground habanero in the batter.

Fish:

> 2 pounds red snapper, fillets or cut into fingers
>
> 2 limes, cut in half
>
> 1 tablespoon habanero hot sauce, such as
>   West Indies Pepper Sauce (page 44)
>
> 2 cloves garlic, minced
>
> 2 green onions, minced
>
> 1 cup all-purpose flour
>
> 2 tablespoons cornstarch
>
> 1 teaspoon ground ginger
>
> 1 teaspoon salt
>
> ½ teaspoon ground dried habanero
>
> ¼ teaspoon white pepper
>
> 1 egg
>
> vegetable oil, for deep-frying

Relish:

> 1 purple onion, sliced
>
> 1 yellow onion, sliced
>
> 1 tablespoon honey
>
> 2 tablespoons red wine vinegar
>
> 2 tablespoons dry red wine

To prepare the fish, rub the fish with the cut limes. In a small bowl, stir together the hot sauce, garlic, and green onion and rub the mixture onto the fish. Place the fish in a nonreactive dish, cover, and refrigerate for at least 2 hours. The fish can either be left whole or cut into "fingers" (strips).

Stir together the flour, cornstarch, ginger, salt, ground chile, and white pepper in a shallow bowl. Lightly beat the egg in another shallow bowl.

Pour oil into a deep skillet to a depth of 2 inches. Heat to 370°F.

Dip the fish in the egg and then into the flour mixture, shaking off any excess. Working in batches, slip the fish into the oil and fry until golden brown and crispy. Remove and keep warm.

To make the relish, pour off all but 1 tablespoon of the oil from the pan. Add the onions to the pan and sauté until soft. Stir in the honey and continue to sauté until the onions have caramelized. Add the vinegar and wine and reduce the sauce to thicken slightly.

To serve, if the fish is whole, place on a platter and top with the onion relish. If the fish is cut into fingers, arrange on a bed of the onion relish on a platter and top with the fish.

Yield: 4 servings

Peppers at the Central Market, Port of Spain, Trinidad.

Baked Red Snapper with Island Fruit Salsa Stuffing

We've included a salsa to use for the stuffing, but other salsas can be used. The Pineapple-Habanero Salsa (page 48) or the Tropical Fruit Salsa (page 99) would be delicious.

Salsa:

- 1 large grapefruit, cut into segments
- 2 oranges, cut into segments
- 1 mango, peeled and diced
- ½ cup cooked tiny shrimp
- ¼ cup diced purple onion
- 1 habanero, seeds and stem removed, minced
- 2 tablespoons chopped fresh cilantro
- 1 teaspoon olive oil

Red Snapper:

- 1 red snapper, 3 to 4 pounds, cleaned
- 6 to 8 slices bacon
- 2 tablespoons margarine or butter, melted
- 1 lemon thinly sliced
- salt and freshly ground black pepper, to taste

Preheat an oven to 350°F.

To make the stuffing, in a bowl, gently toss together all the ingredients.

Spoon the stuffing into the fish cavity and secure the cavity closed with toothpicks. Wrap the bacon slices around the fish, covering completely, and place the fish in an oiled baking dish. Pour the remaining melted butter over the top and then arrange the lemon slices over the fish.

Bake uncovered until fish flakes easily when tested with a fork, basting occasionally with pan juices, 40 to 45 minutes.

Allow to sit for 5 minutes before serving.

Yield: 4 servings

Charbroiled Halibut Steaks with Salsa de Aguacate

The hot and rich avocado sauce perfectly complements the flavor of the fish in this recipe, but it is delectable with chicken as well. Because the sauce is so rich, simple accompaniments, such as a plain rice or potatoes and a vegetable are all that are needed.

Salsa:
  3 fresh or canned tomatillos
  2 avocados, chopped
  2 habaneros, seeds and stems removed, minced
  4 cloves garlic, chopped
  I small onion chopped
  2 teaspoons fresh lime juice
  salt, to taste

  4 halibut steaks, ½ to ¾ inch thick
  chopped fresh cilantro, for garnish

Prepare a fire in a charcoal grill.

To make the salsa, if using fresh tomatillos, remove the husks and place the tomatillos in a small saucepan with a little water. Simmer until they turn light green and are soft, 10 to 15 minutes. Drain.

If using canned tomatillos, simply drain them. Place ingredients, except the salt, in a blender or food processor. Purée, adding a little water if needed to make the sauce smooth and creamy. Taste and add salt, if needed.

Place the halibut steaks on the grill rack and grill, turning once, until they flake easily when tested with a fork.

To serve, place the steaks on individual plates and drizzle the salsa over the top. Garnish with the cilantro and serve.

Yield: 4 servings

Camarones de Infierno

These "shrimps from hell" were created at the Zócalo restaurant in Philadelphia by chef Jackie Pestka. The recipe was first published in *Chile Pepper* magazine. The secret to making it fresh is to use never-frozen shrimp.

12 large shrimp, peeled and deveined with heads and
    tails intact

2 tablespoons vegetable oil

4 cloves garlic, minced

I teaspoon minced habanero

I teaspoon minced fresh cayenne or piquin chile

I teaspoon minced serrano chile

I teaspoon fresh lime juice

¼ cup dry white wine

2 tablespoons butter or margarine

I cup cooked white rice

chopped fresh cilantro, for garnish

In a skillet, sauté the shrimp in the oil, tossing constantly, just until they turn pink, about 3 to 5 minutes. Add the garlic, all the chiles, lime juice, and wine. Toss briefly.

Remove from the heat and add the butter, a little at a time, stirring until an emulsion is formed.

Serve over white rice with the cilantro as a garnish.

Yield: 2 servings
❦ EXTREMELY HOT

Caribbean Stuffed Crab Backs

Here's a recipe that's popular at shoreside restaurants in Tobago. The crabs there are the large blue variety, but any crab of a similar size will work. A chilled white wine and tossed green salad are all that you need to make a truly elegant lunch.

> 2 tablespoons chopped green onions
> 2 habaneros, seeds and stems removed, minced
> 3 tablespoons butter or margarine
> 4 crabs, I pound each, split open, meat removed,
>   and shells reserved
> 2 tablespoons coconut milk or heavy cream
> 3 tablespoons chopped fresh chives
> I tablespoon fresh lime juice
> 2 tablespoons dark rum
> ½ teaspoons ground cloves
> ¼ teaspoon ground nutmeg
> ¼ teaspoon whole celery seeds
> salt and freshly ground black pepper, to taste
> 2 cups fresh bread crumbs

Preheat an oven to 350°F.

In a skillet, sauté the onions and habanero in 1 tablespoon of the butter until soft. Remove from the heat.

In a bowl, combine the crab meat, sautéed onion mixture, coconut milk, chives, lime juice, rum, cloves, nutmeg, celery seeds, salt and pepper, and 1¾ cups of the bread crumbs. Mix thoroughly. Spoon the filling into the reserved shells and place the shells, filling side up, in a baking dish. Bake for 15 minutes.

Sprinkle the remaining bread crumbs over the crab mixture and then dot with remaining butter. Return to the oven and bake until golden brown, 15 to 20 minutes.

Yield: 4 servings

Seafood Tacos

Seafood tacos, which are a pleasant change from the more common chicken, beef, or bean varieties, are sold along the coasts of Mexico. Various seafoods, including shrimp, scallops, or even chopped squid or octopus, can be used in place of the white fish.

Salsa:
- 1 cup chopped mango
- 2 fresh or canned tomatillos, husks removed if fresh, and coarsely chopped
- ¼ cup chopped onion
- 1 habanero, seeds and stem removed, chopped
- ½ teaspoon ground cinnamon
- 2 tablespoons vegetable oil
- 1 tablespoon fresh orange juice

Filling:
- 1 pound white fish, cooked and flaked
- 1 small onion, chopped or thinly sliced
- 1 cup finely shredded cabbage
- 1 cup grated Monterey Jack cheese
- chopped fresh cilantro

- vegetable oil, for frying
- 6 to 8 corn tortillas

To make the salsa, place all the ingredients in a blender or food processor and purée until smooth.

To make the filling, combine all the ingredients in a bowl and toss gently to mix well.

In a small skillet, pour in oil to a depth of ½ inch, heat, and fry the tortillas for a couple of seconds to soften. Drain and fold in half.

Stuff each taco shell with some of the filling and arrange on a platter with salsa on the side.

Yield: 6 to 8

Braised Monkfish
with Gingered Fruit Cream

It's fitting that such a rich sauce should accompany the fish that has been labeled the poor man's lobster. The richness comes from the coconut cream, which is unsweetened thick coconut milk that is found in cans in Asian markets. Do not use the sweet piña colada mix that is also made from coconut cream. Serve this dish with simple side dishes, such as Spice-Up Rice and Peas (page 135).

1½ pounds monkfish, cut into 1-inch cubes
all-purpose flour, for dredging
3 tablespoons vegetable oil
1½ tablespoons grated fresh ginger
1 cup dry white wine
2 Scotch bonnets, seeds and stems removed, chopped
10 dried apricot halves, chopped
10 dried peach halves, chopped
¼ cup golden raisins soaked in 2 tablespoons Grand
    Marnier or Curaçao
½ cup coconut cream

Spread flour on a plate and dredge the fish cubes in it, shaking off any excess. In a skillet, fry the cubes in the oil until browned. Remove the cubes to a plate, and keep warm.

Add the ginger to the skillet and sauté for a couple of minutes. Pour in the wine, raise the heat, and deglaze the pan, scraping up any browned bits. Add the chiles, dried fruits, and the raisins and their liqueur. Simmer until the fruits have plumped, about 5 minutes. Stir in the coconut cream and return the fish to the pan. Heat through and transfer to a serving dish.

Yield: 4 servings

Grilled Scallops with a Rocotillo Mango Relish

Chris Schlesinger, of the East Coast Grill in Cambridge, Massachusetts, sent us this recipe, which was published in an early issue of *Chile Pepper* magazine. The sharp spiciness (not heat) of the chile combines easily with the mellow sweetness of the mango to create a strong but not overpowering accompaniment to the creamy scallops. If using bamboo skewers, immerse them in water and soak for 20 minutes to prevent them from burning on the grill.

I cup *rocotillo* chiles or 3 habaneros, seeds and stems removed, minced
I small purple onion, diced
I green bell pepper, seeds, ribs, and stem removed, diced
I red bell pepper, seeds, ribs and stem removed, diced
2 ripe mangoes, peeled, pitted, and diced
juice of 3 oranges
½ cup pineapple juice, fresh preferred
juice of 4 limes
¼ cup chopped fresh cilantro
2 pounds sea scallops
salt and freshly ground black pepper, to taste

Prepare a fire in a charcoal grill.

In a bowl, combine all the ingredients except scallops, salt, and pepper. Mix well.

Bring a saucepan filled with water to a boil, add the scallops, and blanch 1½ minutes. Drain, pat dry, and sprinkle with salt and pepper.

Thread the scallops onto skewers. Grill over medium-hot coals, turning once, until golden brown on the outside and opaque throughout, 2 to 3 minutes on each side.

Make a bed of the relish on each plate. Place the grilled scallops on top and serve.

Yield: 4 to 6 servings
EXTREMELY HOT

Poblanos with Hot Shrimp and Goat Cheese Filling

The sharpness of the goat cheese makes it an interesting stuffing for the poblano chiles. If poblanos are unavailable, New Mexican chiles can be substituted. Other seafood will work as well.

4 shallots minced

2 cloves garlic, minced

I tablespoon grated fresh ginger

2 habaneros, seeds and stems removed, minced

I tablespoon butter or margarine

½ pound cooked shrimp, shelled and deveined

I tablespoon fresh lime juice

2 cups grated sharp goat cheese

3 tablespoons chopped fresh cilantro

4 poblano chiles, roasted and peeled (see Glossary)

all-purpose flour, for dredging

vegetable oil, for deep-frying

Batter:

3 eggs, separated

I tablespoon water

3 tablespoons all purpose flour

¼ teaspoon salt

In a skillet, sauté the shallots, garlic, ginger and habaneros in the butter until soft. Transfer to a bowl and add the shrimp, lime juice, cheese, and cilantro. Toss well.

Make a slit in the side of each poblano chile. Divide the shrimp mixture evenly among the chiles, stuffing them carefully to avoid tearing. Dredge the stuffed chiles in the flour, shaking off any excess. Set aside.

To make the batter, beat the egg whites in a bowl until they form stiff peaks. In another bowl, beat the yolks with the water, flour, and salt until thick and creamy. Fold the yolks into the whites.

Pour oil into a deep skillet to a depth of 2 to 3 inches and heat to 370°. Dip the chiles into the batter, coating completely, then slip them into the oil. Fry until golden brown. Remove to paper towels to drain.

Yield: 4 servings

Asian Pineapple Tuna Steaks

Grilling is a wonderful, quick way to prepare fish and this recipe is no exception. The spicy sauce is also good on halibut or salmon steaks, as well as on poultry, pork, and grilled vegetables.

> **2 teaspoons sesame oil**
> **½ cup rice vinegar**
> **3 tablespoons rice wine or dry sherry**
> **2 tablespoons soy sauce**
> **1½ teaspoons minced habanero**
> **¼ teaspoon five-spice powder**
> **1 cup chicken broth**
> **¼ cup chopped green onion, including the green tops**
> **1 tablespoon minced fresh ginger**
> **2 tablespoons peanut oil**
> **1 tablespoon cornstarch mixed with 2 tablespoons water**
> **4 tuna steaks, 1 to 1½ inches thick**
> **4 pineapple rings**

Prepare a fire in a charcoal grill.

In a bowl, combine the sesame oil, vinegar, wine, soy sauce, chile, five-spice powder, and chicken broth. Mix well.

In a skillet, sauté the green onion and ginger in the peanut oil for 1 minute. Add the sesame oil mixture and bring to a boil. Slowly stir in the cornstarch mixture and simmer, stirring, until the sauce has thickened, a couple of minutes.

Place the tuna steaks in a grill rack and brush with the sauce. Grill, turning once, and brushing with more sauce, about 2 minutes on each side. A couple of minutes before the fish is done, place the pineapple rings on the grill, brush with the sauce, and heat through.

To serve, place a pineapple ring on top of each steak. Serve the sauce on the side.

Yield: 4 servings

Martinique Crab Rice with Wine

This easy-to-prepare Creole-style dish is best served accompanied with green beans and a tossed salad.

½ cup chopped green bell pepper

1 green onion, including the green tops, chopped

1 clove garlic, minced

6 *rocotillos* or 2 habaneros, seeds and stems removed, chopped

3 tablespoons olive oil

1½ cups white rice

3 tomatoes, peeled and chopped

2 tablespoons tomato paste

½ teaspoon dried oregano

2 bay leaves

1½ cups cooked crab meat

2 cups chicken broth

1 cup dry white wine

2 tablespoons chopped fresh parsley

In a skillet, sauté the bell pepper, green onion, garlic, and chiles in the oil until soft. Add the rice and continue to sauté until the rice browns slightly.

In a dutch oven, combine all the remaining ingredients except the parsley. Bring to a boil and pour in the rice mixture. Stir once and bring back to a boil. Reduce the heat, cover, and simmer until the rice is tender, about 30 minutes.

Fluff the rice with a fork and remove and discard the bay leaves. Garnish with the parsley and serve.

Yield: 4 servings

Escovitch Fish

This Caribbean-style pickled fish is similar to Spanish *escabeche*. Highly versatile, it can be served hot or cold or as a main course or an appetizer.

Fish:

> 2 pounds fish fillets or steaks, such as king mackerel, grouper, or other firm, highly flavored fish
>
> juice of I lime
>
> Dry Jerk Rub Seasoning (page 50)
>
> ¼ cup olive oil

Pickling Mixture:

> 2 carrots, peeled and thinly sliced
>
> I small red bell pepper, seeds, ribs, and stem removed, cut into thin strips
>
> I purple onion, thinly sliced
>
> 2 Scotch bonnets, seeds and stems removed, cut into thin strips
>
> 2 yellow wax, banana, or other mild chiles, seeds, and stems removed, cut into thin strips
>
> 2 cloves garlic
>
> I tablespoon whole pimento berries (or ½ tablespoon ground allspice)
>
> ¾ cup malt or apple cider vinegar
>
> 2 tablespoons dry white wine
>
> I tablespoon drained capers

Place the fish fillets on a plate and rub both sides with the lime juice. Liberally sprinkle both sides of the fish with the jerk seasoning.

In a skillet over high heat, heat the olive oil until it is very hot. Add the fish and fry, turning, until browned on both sides. Using a slotted utensil, remove the fish to a nonreactive dish.

To make the pickling mixture, in a saucepan, combine the carrots, bell pepper, onion, chiles, garlic, pimento berries, vinegar, wine, and some of the oil from frying the fish. Bring to a boil and boil for 3 minutes. Remove from the heat and pour the hot pickling mixture over the fish.

The fish can be served warm at this point. Or, allow the fish to cool, cover, refrigerate, and let marinate for up to 3 days in the refrigerator.

Yield: 4 servings

Vatapa

Vatapá de camarao e peixe is a traditional Brazilian seafood stew. Normally it's extremely high in saturated fat because it is cooked with coconut milk and *dende* (palm) oil. The fat content can be lowered, however, by using the new reduced-fat coconut milk now on the market and by adding paprika for color in place of the *dende* oil.

2 pounds white fish fillets, cut into 1½-inch cubes
1 pound shrimp, peeled and deveined
3 tablespoons olive oil
1 onion, chopped
1 tablespoon minced garlic
1 *pimenta do cheiro*, seeds and stems removed, chopped
2 tomatoes, peeled and chopped
juice of 1 lemon
⅓ cup lowfat coconut milk
2 cups chicken broth
2 teaspoons paprika
¼ cup ground cashews
2 tablespoons chopped fresh cilantro
chopped fresh cilantro, toasted grated coconut, and
**   coarsely chopped cashews, for garnish**

In a dutch oven, sauté the fish and shrimp in the oil until just cooked, about 2½ minutes. Remove to a bowl and keep warm.

Add the onion and garlic to the same pan and sauté until the onion is soft. Add the chile and tomatoes and simmer for a couple of minutes. Add the lemon juice, cover, and cook for 5 minutes.

Stir in the coconut milk, broth, paprika, ground cashews, and the 2 tablespoons cilantro. Bring to a boil, reduce the heat, and simmer uncovered, until the sauce is thickened, about 15 minutes.

Return the fish and shrimp to the pan and heat through. Garnish with cilantro, coconut, and chopped cashews.

Yield: 6 servings

Deviled Crab Cakes with
Tangy Mustard Sauce

Don't let the long list of ingredients intimidate you, because this is not a difficult recipe. The cakes can be made large or small, depending on how you wish to serve them—as an appetizer or an entrée. *NOTE: The crab mixture must be well chilled before forming the cakes, so allow a few hours for this step.*

Crab Cakes:
- 1 cup chopped green bell pepper
- 1 cup chopped onion
- 1 teaspoon finely chopped garlic
- 2 Scotch bonnets, seeds and stems removed, chopped
- 3 tablespoons butter or margarine
- 1 cup dry white wine
- ½ cup fresh bread crumbs, or as needed
- 2 eggs, lightly beaten
- ½ cup heavy cream
- 1 tablespoon Island Sherry Sauce (page 43)
- 1 tablespoon fresh lemon juice
- ½ teaspoon salt
- ½ teaspoon whole pimento berries
  (or ¼ teaspoon ground allspice)
- pinch of ground cloves
- 2 tablespoons chopped fresh parsley
- 1 pound crab meat

Sauce:
- ½ cup dry white wine
- ½ cup chicken broth
- ½ cup heavy cream
- 2 tablespoons Dijon-style mustard
- 1 tablespoon Island Sherry Sauce (page 43)
- ½ teaspoon chopped fresh tarragon

- vegetable oil, for deep-frying
- 1 cup fine dried bread crumbs
- 1 egg beaten with 1 tablespoon water

In a skillet, sauté the bell pepper, onion, garlic, and chiles in the butter until soft. Add the wine, bring to a boil, and boil, stirring frequently, until the wine is almost evaporated. Remove from the heat and stir in the ½ cup bread crumbs.

In a bowl, combine the eggs, cream, sherry sauce, lemon juice, salt, pimento berries, cloves, parsley, and crab meat. Add the sautéed mixture, adding more bread crumbs if necessary to hold the mixture together. Cover and chill in the refrigerator for 2 to 3 hours.

To make the sauce, combine the wine, broth, and cream in a small saucepan. Simmer until reduced by half. Remove from the heat and stir in the mustard, sherry sauce, and tarragon.

In a deep skillet or a saucepan, pour oil to a depth of 2 inches. Heat the oil to 375°F.

Meanwhile, shape the crab mixture into cakes, about 3 inches in diameter. Spread the bread crumbs on a plate and whisk together the egg and water in a shallow bowl. Coat the cakes with the crumbs, dip them in the egg, then coat with the crumbs again. Allow to dry for 10 minutes.

Fry the cakes until golden, remove, and drain on paper towels. Serve with the mustard sauce on the side.

Yield: 6 servings

Habaneros for sale.

West Indies Pepper Shrimp

Hot and sweet and quick and easy, this shrimp recipe is one of our favorites. Serve with a rice pilaf and a green vegetable, such as broccoli or and an appetizer to a meal of grilled steaks or lamb chops.

> ¼ cup vegetable oil
>
> 2 Scotch bonnets, seeds and stems removed, minced
>
> 2 tablespoons fresh lemon juice
>
> 2 tablespoons honey
>
> 3 tablespoons West Indies Pepper Sauce (page 44) or
> other fruit-based habanero hot sauce
>
> 1 pound large shrimp, peeled and deveined
>
> lemon wedges, for garnish

In a skillet, sauté the chiles for 1 minute. Stir in the lemon juice, honey, and pepper sauce. Add the shrimp, toss to coat, and transfer the mixture to a baking dish. Let marinate at room temperature for 1 hour.

Preheat an oven to 450°F.

Bake the shrimp, stirring occasionally, until they are cooked, 5 to 8 minutes.

Garnish with the lemon wedges, and serve.

Yield: 2 to 4 servings
♥ EXTREMELY HOT

Belizean habanero.

Pescado Sobre Uso

Rodolfo de Gary and Thomas Brown reported on some surprisingly spicy Cuban delicacies for *Chile Pepper* magazine. The name of this dish, which translates as "*sofrito* for reused fish," may not sound too appetizing, but when faced with a lack of refrigeration, this recipe solves the problem: the entire catch of fish is cooked immediately and then eaten later. *Sofrito* refers to the mixture of onion, tomatoes, peppers, and spices, in a basic sauce that is used in Spanish dishes.

> **6 white fish fillets, such as snapper or grouper**
>
> **3 tablespoons olive oil**
>
> **I large onion, sliced and separated into rings**
>
> **10 *rocotillos*, stems removed, cut in half and seeds removed, or 2 habaneros and 5 yellow wax chiles**
>
> **½ cup chopped *cubanelles* or I bell pepper**
>
> **5 cloves garlic, minced**
>
> **I teaspoon dried oregano**
>
> **¼ teaspoon freshly ground black pepper**
>
> **I tablespoon white vinegar**

In a skillet, fry the fish fillets in the oil until they are slightly browned and cooked, about 3 minutes per side. Remove and keep warm. Strain the oil and return it to the skillet.

Reheat the oil and sauté the onions until soft. Add the chiles, garlic, oregano, and black pepper and cook, stirring for 4 minutes. Stir in the vinegar and remove from the heat.

Using a slotted spoon, ladle the *sofrito* over the fillets and serve.

Yield: 6 servings

Piling on the Heat: Vegetables, Rice, and Other Accompaniments

Here is a wide variety of highly spiced side dishes. We realize that we will be accused of culinary overkill when we recommend serving habanero-infused accompaniments along with pungent appetizers, soups, salads, and main courses. But not every course of every meal needs to be fiery. Serve some of these dishes to balance blander fare, such as grilled or roasted meats.

How about an Avocado-Herb Omelet with Hot Chutney to start the day off? One of the most typical Caribbean accompaniments is rice, and we've fired up some wonderful rice dishes, such as Spiced-Up Rice and Peas and Belizean Coconut Rice. Other favorite ingredients for making side dishes with a bite include black beans (Cuban Frijoles Negros and Black Beans with Squash and Cashews), potatoes (West Indian Shrimp-and-Potato Fritters and Papas a la Huancaina), vegetables (Creole Ratatouille and Carrots and Chayote with Lemon Glaze), onion (Cebollas con Habanero), and bread (Spiced Pumpkin Muffins and Curried Roti). Enjoy your trip to habanero heaven!

Avocado-Herb Omelet with Hot Chutney

Paul and Melba Vigneault, our hosts at the Hotel Jaguar, outside of Limón, Costa Rica, served their wonderful omelet garnished with slices of red-skinned avocado for breakfast. When Paul makes his chutney, he doesn't like to use sugar. Instead he uses the flavor of fresh fruit to sweeten his chutneys and sauces naturally.

Chutney:
- 2 tomatoes, peeled and chopped
- 3 cups diced papaya
- 2 tablespoons raisins
- 1 habanero, seeds and stem removed, minced

Omelet:
- 1 large avocado
- ¼ cup minced onion
- 4 eggs
- 2 tablespoons chopped fresh cilantro
- 1 habanero, seeds and stems removed, minced
- 2 tablespoons olive oil
- cilantro leaves, for garnish

To make the chutney, in a large skillet, combine all the ingredients and simmer gently until the tomatoes have broken down and the sauce has thickened, 20 to 30 minutes.

To make the omelet, in a bowl, mash the avocado and then mix in the onion. In another bowl, beat 2 of the eggs until blended. Beat in half of the cilantro and half of the chiles.

Heat 1 tablespoon of oil in an omelet pan over high heat. Pour the beaten eggs into the pan and scramble them, moving the pan at the same time, until the mixture starts to thicken. Spoon half of the avocado mixture onto one half of the omelet and allow the omelet to finish cooking.

Run a spatula or knife around the edges of the omelet to make sure it doesn't stick to the pan. Tip the pan upward so the eggs slide toward the front and then fold the set eggs over the filling to cover.

Turn the omelet out onto a plate. Garnish with avocado slices and a few cilantro leaves. Repeat with the remaining ingredients to make a second omelet. Serve the chutney on the side.

Yield: 2 servings

Spiced-Up Rice and Peas

Rice and peas (or beans) are eaten throughout the Caribbean. Perhaps the popularity is based on the fact that eating rice helps tame the fire of hot foods. The peas used in this recipe are called pigeon peas. They are about the size of garden peas and are available dried or in cans. Kidney, red, or black beans can be substituted.

> ½ cup dried pigeon peas, washed and picked over, or
>   1 can (8 ounces) pigeon peas
> 1 Scotch bonnet, seeds and stem removed, chopped
> 2 cloves garlic, minced
> 1 onion, chopped
> 2 tablespoons vegetable oil
> 2 cups rice
> 1 cup coconut milk
> 2 green onions, chopped

If using dried peas, place in a large saucepan and add water to cover. Bring to a boil, reduce the heat and cook until tender, about 30 minutes.

In a dutch oven, sauté the garlic, chile, and onion in the oil until soft. Add the rice and continue to sauté until the rice browns slightly. Stir the peas into the rice.

In a saucepan, combine the coconut milk with 3 cups of the bean liquid. (If you do not have enough bean liquid, add water to make up the difference.) Bring to a boil and add the rice mixture. Bring the liquid back to a boil and immediately reduce the heat to low. Cover and simmer until the liquid is absorbed and the rice is tender, 20 to 25 minutes.

Fluff the rice with a fork, stir in the green onions, and serve.

Yield: 6 servings

Belizean Coconut Rice

Coconuts are plentiful in Belize—in fact, Nancy almost got beaned on the head by one while sitting on the porch during our stay—so we tried to use them as much as we could in our cooking.

I habanero, seeds and stem removed, chopped
I cup finely chopped or coarsely grated fresh coconut
2 tablespoons butter or margarine
I small onion, finely chopped
I cup white rice
I cup coconut water (from the coconut)
I cup chicken broth

In a saucepan, sauté the chile and coconut in the butter until it starts to brown, for a couple of minutes. Add the onion and sauté until the onion is soft.

Stir in the rice and continue to sauté until the rice turns opaque.

In another saucepan, combine the coconut milk and broth, bring to a boil, and add the rice mixture. Bring the liquid back to a boil and immediately reduce the heat to low. Cover and cook until the liquid is absorbed and the rice is tender, 20 to 25 minutes.

Yield: 4 to 6 servings

Wild Brazilian *chinense*.

Cuban Frijoles Negros

Black beans are a staple in the Cuban diet and are prepared in a variety of ways. Serve these with plain white rice.

> **2 cups dried black beans**
>
> **6 *rocotillos*, 2 whole and 4 with seeds and stems removed and chopped or 2 habaneros, I whole and I chopped**
>
> **2 bay leaves**
>
> **2 onions, I coarsely chopped and I diced**
>
> **I small green bell pepper, seeds ribs, and stem removed, chopped**
>
> **2 cloves garlic, minced**
>
> **2 tablespoons olive oil**
>
> **I cup chopped canned tomatoes, with juice**
>
> **I teaspoon ground cumin**
>
> **2 tablespoons red wine vinegar**
>
> **salt and freshly ground black pepper, to taste**

In a large saucepan, combine the beans with water to cover. Add the whole *rocotillos*. Coarsely chop 1 of the onions and add that as well. Let sit overnight.

Remove the *rocotillos* and discard. Add water to cover, if necesssary and the bay leaves and bring to a boil. Reduce the heat to low and simmer until the beans are almost done, about 2 hours. Remove and discard the bay leaves.

Sauté the diced onion, bell pepper, and garlic in the oil until they start to soften. Add to the beans, along with the tomato and cumin. Continue to simmer the beans for 30 minutes.

Add the remaining chopped *rocotillos* along with vinegar, and salt and pepper. Simmer until the beans are tender, 20 to 30 minutes.

Yield: 6 to 8 servings

Pasta from Hell

This is one of the all-time favorite habanero recipes published in *Chile Pepper* magazine. Chris Schlesinger, of the East Coast Grill in Cambridge, Massachusetts, who invented the recipe describes it this way: "This dish is on the outer limits. Constantly challenged by my heat-seeking customers to create hotter and hotter food, I decided to put a stop to it once and for all by developing a dish that would satisfy their desires and quiet their demands. A dish that was so hot that there was no hotter, so hot that never again would I have to take a ribbing from the heat freaks. This is it." Needless to say, it is extremely hot.

I red bell pepper, seeds, ribs, and stem removed, diced
I onion, diced
2 tablespoons olive oil
2 teaspoons butter or margarine
2 bananas, sliced
¼ cup pineapple juice, fresh preferred
juice of 3 oranges
juice of 2 limes
¼ cup chopped fresh cilantro
3 to 4 tablespoons minced habanero
4 tablespoons grated Parmesan cheese
I pound dried fettucine
salt and freshly ground black pepper, to taste

In a large skillet, sauté the bell pepper and onion in the oil and butter until soft, about 4 minute. Add the bananas and pineapple and orange juices and continue to simmer until the bananas are soft, about 4 minutes. Remove from the heat and add the lime juice, cilantro, chile, and 3 tablespoons of the cheese. Mix well.

Meanwhile, bring a large pot filled with water to a boil and add the fettucine. Cook until *al dente*, 8 to 10 minutes.

Place the fettucine on a platter and top with the hot fruit sauce. Sprinkle with the remaining tablespoon of cheese, season with salt and pepper, and serve.

Yield: 4 servings
❦ EXTREMELY HOT

West Indian Shrimp-and-Potato Fritters

These fritters make a tasty side dish. To spice them up further, serve with
Pawpaw Pepper Mustard (page 55).

2 cups mashed cooked potatoes
I small onion, minced
2 tablespoons minced cilantro
I cup grated Cheddar cheese
4 tablespoons butter or margarine, cut into small pieces
I egg yolk, plus 2 whole eggs
2 teaspoons minced Scotch bonnets
¼ pound shrimp, cooked, peeled, deveined, and chopped
all-purpose flour, for dredging
½ cup fine dried bread crumbs
vegetable oil, for deep-frying

Combine the potatoes, onion, cilantro, and cheese in a bowl. Mix
well. Add the butter, egg yolk, and chile and stir to combine thoroughly. Pinch off 2 to 3 tablespoons of the potato mixture and shape into
round patties, about 2½ inches in diameter. Spread flour on a plate. Lightly
beat the whole eggs in a shallow bowl and put the bread crumbs in a
separate bowl. Dredge the patties in the flour, shaking off any excess.
Then dip them in the eggs and finally in the bread crumbs, coating completely. Place the coated patties on a large plate or tray. Cover and refrigerate for 30 minutes.

Pour oil into a deep skillet to a depth of 4 inches and heat to 375°F.
Working in batches, slip the patties into the oil and fry until golden,
about 4 minutes. Remove to paper towels and drain. Serve warm.

Yield: 4 to 6 servings

Papas a la Huancaína

Here's a traditional hot and spicy dish from the land that gave the world potatoes, Peru. These cheese-topped potatoes give a double kick—one from the marinated onions and the other from the cheese sauce. Often *ají* chiles are used, but we've opted for the hotter habanero here.

½ cup fresh lemon juice

½ teaspoon crushed dried habanero chile

¼ teaspoon salt

1 large onion, sliced and separated into rings,
    plus ½ cup chopped onion

2 small habaneros, seeds and stems removed, chopped

1 tablespoon olive oil

½ cup evaporated milk

¼ cup heavy cream

¼ cup dry sherry

½ teaspoon ground turmeric

½ cup grated *queso blanco* or mozzarella cheese

4 potatoes, peeled, boiled until tender, cooled, and diced

sliced black olives

Combine the lemon juice, chile, salt, and onion rings in a bowl and toss until the rings are coated. Cover and marinate at room temperature for 30 minutes.

In a skillet, sauté the chopped onion and chiles in the oil until soft. Transfer to a blender or food processor and add the evaporated milk. Process until a smooth sauce forms. Strain, if necessary.

Pour the sauce into a saucepan. Stir in the cream, sherry, turmeric, and cheese. Simmer, stirring constantly, until the cheese melts and the sauce has thickened, about 5 minutes.

Drain the marinated onion rings. Place the potatoes on a serving platter and pour the sauce over the top. Garnish with the onion rings and black olives and serve.

Yield: 4 to 6 servings

Creole Ratatouille

This spicy variation on the classic Mediterranean dish is almost a meal in itself. If chayote is unavailable in your area, substitute the more traditional zucchini.

> 2 habaneros, seeds and stems removed, minced
>
> I large onion, thinly sliced
>
> 2 celery stalk, diced
>
> 3 green onions, including the green tops, chopped
>
> 2 cloves garlic, minced
>
> 2 tablespoons olive oil
>
> I eggplant, peeled and cut into 2-inch-wide, 3-inch-long strips
>
> I red bell pepper, seeds, ribs, and stem removed, cut into 2-inch-wide strips
>
> I chayote, peeled, seeded, and chopped
>
> 3 tomatoes, roasted, peeled, seeded, and chopped
>
> I tablespoon minced fresh basil, plus basil leaves, for garnish
>
> 2 teaspoons dried thyme
>
> I teaspoon brown sugar
>
> salt and freshly ground black pepper, to taste
>
> I cup dry white wine

Preheat an oven to 375°F.

In a skillet, sauté the chiles, onions, celery, green onions, and garlic in the oil for 5 minutes. Remove the onion mixture to a plate. Add the eggplant to the same pan and sauté, turning, until browned.

Layer the eggplant, bell pepper, chayote, tomatoes, and onion mixture in a casserole. Sprinkle each layer with the basil, thyme, sugar, and salt and black pepper. Combine the wine and water and pour evenly over the top.

Bake uncovered for 30 to 45 minutes.

Taste and adjust the seasoning. Garnish with basil leaves and serve either hot or at room temperature.

Yield: 4 to 6 servings

Marinated Grilled Vegetables

Serve these spicy vegetables as a side dish to just about any grilled meat or fish. If using bamboo skewers, soak them in water for 20 minutes to prevent them from burning on the grill.

Vegetables:

- 8 cherry tomatoes, halved
- 1 green bell pepper, seeds, ribs, and stem removed, cut lengthwise into wedges
- 8 large mushrooms
- 1 onion, cut into wedges and separated
- 1 zucchini, scored with a fork and cut into ½-inch-thick slices

Marinade:

- 6 green onions, minced
- 1 Scotch bonnet, seeds and stem removed, minced
- ½ cup soy sauce
- ½ cup malt vinegar
- ¼ cup vegetable oil
- 2 tablespoons fresh lime juice
- 2 tablespoons chopped fresh thyme
- ½ teaspoon ground cloves
- ½ teaspoon ground nutmeg
- ½ teaspoon ground allspice
- ¼ teaspoon ground cinnamon

To prepare the vegetables, thread them onto skewers, alternating colors and shapes, and place in a baking dish.

To make the marinade, in a bowl combine all the ingredients and pour over the vegetables. Marinate for 2 to 3 hours, spooning the marinade over the vegetables occasionally.

Prepare a fire in a charcoal grill. Brush the grill rack with oil. Grill the vegetables for 3 to 5 minutes, or until the vegetables are cooked but still crisp, basting frequently with the marinade.

Yield: 4 to 6 servings

Black Beans with Squash and Cashews

This colorful accompaniment could also be served as a vegetarian entrée. Feel free to substitute pistachios, pine nuts, or macadamia nuts for the cashews.

> 4 leeks, white part only, thinly sliced
> I clove garlic, minced
> 2 cups cubed, peeled butternut or acorn squash, cut into I-inch cubes
> I Scotch bonnet, seeds and stem removed, chopped
> 2 tablespoons olive oil
> ¼ cup dry sherry
> ¼ cup chicken broth
> 2 cups cooked and drained black beans
> ½ teaspoon dried thyme
> ¼ teaspoon ground cumin
> ¼ teaspoon freshly ground black pepper
> I teaspoon red wine vinegar
> I cup cashews, toasted

In a skillet, sauté the leeks, garlic, squash, and chile in the oil for 5 minutes. Add the sherry and broth and bring to a boil. Reduce the heat and simmer, uncovered, until the squash is tender, about 30 minutes.

Add the beans, thyme, cumin, black pepper, and vinegar. Continue to simmer until the beans are heated through. Stir in the cashews and cook for 1 minute longer.

Yield: 4 servings

Costa Rican red habanero.

Cebollas con Habanero

This recipe, which translates as onions with and habaneros, is great with plain grilled meats. For a truly spectacular presentation, create onion flowers. To make them, peel each onion and cut it in half crosswise, leaving the ends intact. Place each onion half with the end up and out from the top slice into 8 sections each ½ inch deep to within ½ inch of the end, so that the onion half remains intact. The onion will open when baked.

> **3 onions**
> **3 tablespoons red wine vinegar or balsamic vinegar**
> **2 tablespoons butter or margarine, melted**
> **1 tablespoon honey**
> **½ teaspoon ground dried habanero**
> **½ teaspoon salt**

Preheat an oven to 350°F.

Cut the onions as described above and place cut side up in a greased baking pan. In a small bowl, combine the vinegar, butter, honey, chile, and salt and mix well. Brush evenly over the onions.

Bake until the onions are tender, almost 1 hour. Serve hot.

Yield: 6 servings

Carrots and Chayote with Lemon Glaze

Serve this spicy veggie combo with any of the seafood dishes in this book (see pages 111–132).

> **2 large carrots, peeled**
> **1 medium-size chayote, peeled, seeded, and cut into matchstick**
> **3 tablespoons butter or margarine, melted**
> **2 teaspoons fresh lemon juice**
> **1 tablespoon sugar**
> **½ teaspoon chopped fresh datil pepper**
> **1½ cups chicken broth**
> **½ teaspoon grated lemon zest**

Bring a saucepan filled with water to a boil. Add the carrots and blanch for 2 minutes. Drain and plunge the carrots into cold water. Drain again and cut into matchstick-size pieces.

Place the carrots and chayote in single layer in a saucepan. In a bowl, stir together the butter, lemon juice, sugar, and chile and pour over the vegetables. Add the broth and bring to a simmer. Cover and simmer until the vegetables are just done, about 15 minutes. Remove the vegetables to a bowl.

Simmer until the cooking liquid has been reduced to a glaze, 10 to 12 minutes. Return the vegetables to the pan, add the lemon zest, and shake the pan to coat the vegetables with the glaze.

Yield: 4 servings

Sweet and Hot Tropical Beans

Any number of vegetables can be used in this recipe. Substitute carrots, broccoli, snow peas, or a combination of vegetables for the green beans.

> **2 cups sliced green beans**
> **2 cups water or chicken broth**
> **1 cup canned pineapple chunks, with juice**
> **2 tablespoons brown sugar**
> **2 teaspoons soy sauce**
> **2 teaspoons vinegar**
> **½ teaspoon ground dried habanero**
> **¼ cup golden raisins**
> **1 teaspoon cornstarch mixed with 2 tablespoons water**

In a saucepan, combine the green beans and broth and simmer until done but still crisp. Drain, reserving ½ cup of the broth, and keep warm.

Drain the pineapple, reserving the juice. In a saucepan, combine the juice, the reserved broth, brown sugar, soy sauce, vinegar, and chile. Bring to a boil, stirring to dissolve the sugar. Reduce the heat and simmer for 5 minutes. Add the pineapple and raisins and cook for a couple of minutes longer.

Return the green beans to the sauce and heat through. Raise the heat, stir in the cornstarch mixture, and simmer until the sauce has thickened and coats the carrots and fruits.

Yield: 4 servings

Citrus Yuca-Yam Picadillo

Yuca, a long, tuberous root, is served throughout the Caribbean and Central America. It can be found in specialty produce sections or in Latin markets. Yucas tend to be starchy, so we add citrus fruits and juices to cut some of the starch. For a sweeter taste, substitute chopped pineapple for the orange segments.

> **2 cups diced yuca**
> **I cup diced, peeled yam**
> **I small onion, diced**
> **3 cloves garlic, chopped**
> **I habanero, seeds and stem removed, minced**
> **3 tablespoons olive oil**
> **¼ cup fresh orange juice**
> **3 tablespoons fresh lime juice**
> **2 tablespoons chopped fresh parsley**
> **I tablespoon chopped fresh oregano**
> **½ cup chopped orange segments**

In a saucepan, combine the yuca and yam with water to cover. Bring to boil, reduce the heat and simmer until tender, about 20 minutes. Drain and separate the yuca and yam pieces; keep warm.

In a skillet, sauté the onion, garlic, and chile in the oil until soft. Add the juices, orange and lime, parsley, oregano, and yams, and stir well. Rinse the yuca, add to the skillet, and bring the mixture to a simmer, then simmer for 10 minutes. Remove from the heat and stir in the chopped oranges, mixing well.

Yield: 4 to 6 servings

Spiced Pumpkin Muffins

These muffins are so moist and tasty you won't even think about spreading them with butter or margarine. Make a lot and freeze them for future meals.

1¼ cups all-purpose flour
3 teaspoons baking powder
¼ teaspoon salt
½ teaspoon ground cinnamon
½ teaspoon ground dried habanero
¼ teaspoon ground nutmeg
½ cup shortening
¾ cup sugar
2 eggs
1 cup canned pumpkin
½ cup milk
¼ cup raisins

Sugar Topping:
2 tablespoons sugar
½ teaspoon ground cinnamon

Preheat an oven to 375°F. Oil 12 muffin-tin cups.

In a medium bowl, sift together the dry ingredients. Cream the shortening and sugar together until fluffy. Add the eggs, one at a time, beating well after each addition. Beat in the pumpkin, and mix well.

Add one-third of the remaining dry ingredients and mix well.

Combine the sugar and cinnamon.

Spoon the batter into the prepared muffin cups, filling them two-thirds full. Sprinkle the sugar-cinnamon mixture over the top. Bake until a toothpick inserted into the center of a muffin comes out clean, about 20 minutes.

Let cool in muffin tin before turning out.

Yield: 12 muffins

Curried Roti

This West Indies griddle bread is served whole, to be torn for dipping into sauces or left as is for rolling around fillings. We have taken the liberty of adding spices to the traditional recipe.

> 3 cups all-purpose flour
> 1 tablespoon baking powder
> ½ teaspoon salt
> ¼ teaspoon ground cumin
> ¼ teaspoon ground dried habanero
> 1 tablespoon Colombo Curry Paste (page 54)
> 1 cup water
> vegetable oil, for frying

In a bowl, sift the dry ingredients together. Add the curry paste and water and stir to mix well. Knead to form a ball and then let rest for 30 minutes.

Knead the dough again and divide into 6 equal balls.

On a floured work surface, roll out each ball into a round as thin as possible. They should be about 2 inches in diameter.

Pour oil into a heavy skillet until it just barely coats the bottom. Slip the rotis into the pan, being careful not to crowd them, and fry, turning once, until lightly browned, about 1½ minutes each side.

Using tongs or a spatula, remove carefully and drain on paper towels.

Yield: 6

Trinidad seasoning pepper.

GLOSSARY

ají: The common name for chiles in Latin America; usually *Capsicum baccatum*.

bonney pepper: Common name for *C. chinense* in Barbados.

cayenne: A long, thin, hot pod type of *C. annuum*.

chayote: A pear-shaped squash.

chile de árbol: A short, thin pod type of *C. annuum* that is borne erect on the plant.

conch: A shellfish commonly found in Caribbean waters.

coconut milk: Liquid extracted by soaking grated coconut in hot water. Also available canned.

Congo pepper: The common name for *C. chinense* in Trinidad and Tobago.

cubanelle: A long, mild *C. annuum* pod type.

datil pepper: The common name for *C. chinense* in St. Augustine, Florida.

epazote: Known as "Ambrosia" in English, this perennial herb (*Chenopodium ambrosioides*) is strong and bitter and is used primarily to flavor beans.

goat pepper: The common name for *C. chinense* in the Bahamas.

habanero: The common name for *C. chinense* in the Yucatán Peninsula and the United States.

jicama: A white tuber (*Pachyrhizus erosus*) used in salads that tastes like a cross between an apple and a potato.

masa harina: Corn flour

piment bouc: Literally, "goat pepper"; the common name for *C. chinense* in the French Caribbean.

pimenta do cheiro: The common name for *C. chinense* in Brazil.

pimento berries: Allspice.

piquin: A small, extremely hot pod type of *C. annuum*.

plantain: A member of the banana family; must be cooked before eating.

poblano: A large, wide pod type of *C. annuum*; known as "Ancho" in its dried form.

queso blanco: A soft, white cheese from Mexico.

roasting peppers: Using tongs, hold peppers over an open flame until the skin is blistered and blackened. Wrap peppers in wet paper towels and let rest, until skin can be peeled away easily.

roasting tomatoes: Using tongs, hold the tomatoes over an open flame until the skin is blistered and easily removed.

rocotillo: A mild pod type of *C. chinense.*

Scotch bonnet: The common name for *C. chinense* in Jamaica and other parts of the Caribbean.

Seville oranges: A bitter orange grown in the Mediterranean region and in some Latin American countries. As a substitute for the juice, use ½ orange and ½ lime juice.

tamarind sauce: Made by soaking the pulp of tamarind pods in water (see box); also available bottled in Asian markets.

TAMARIND SAUCE

6 tamarind pods

3 cups water

2 tablespoons sugar

Shell the tamarind pods and remove the seeds from the pulp. Bring the water to a boil in a saucepan, add the pulp, and simmer until the liquid is reduced to 1 cup.

Add the sugar, stir to dissolve, and simmer for an additional 5 minutes. Strain the sauce through a piece of cheesecloth or muslin and squeeze out as much liquid as possible from the pulp.

Tamarind Sauce will keep for about a month when stored covered in the refrigerator.

Yield: 2 cups

---

tomatillo: A small, green husk tomato of Mexico and Central America.

yellow wax pepper: A short, medium-hot pod type of *C. annuum.*

APPENDIX:
MAIL-ORDER SOURCES

Seeds and Pods

NOTE: Some of these companies also manufacture and/or sell habanero food products by mail.

Dat'l Do It
P.O. Box 4019
St. Augustine, FL 32084
(800) HOT-DATL

Grower of datil chiles; manufacturer of datil chile products, datil chile seeds.

Enchanted Seeds
P.O Box 6087
Las Cruces, NM 88006
(505) 233-3033

Habanero and other exotic chile seeds.

Frieda's, Inc.
P.O. Box 584888
Los Angeles, CA 90058
(800) 421-9477

Shipper of fresh and dried habaneros.

GNS Spices
P.O. Box 90
Walnut, CA 91788
(909) 594-9505

Grower and shipper of fresh habaneros.

KAL International, Ltd.
P.O. Box 482
Hollis, NH 03049
(603) 465-2428

Importer and distributor of Jamaican Scotch bonnets; manufacturer of Scotch bonnet products.

Los Dos, Inc.
P.O. Box 7548
Albuquerque, NM 87194
(505) 831-9161

Distributor of Rica Red products.

Melissa's World Variety Produce
P.O. Box 21127
Los Angeles, CA 90021
(800) 468-7111

Shipper of fresh, dried, and pickled habaneros.

Pepper Gal
P.O. Box 23006
Fort Lauderdale, FL 33307

Habanero and other *chinense* seeds.

PFM International
   Corporation
2800 N.W. 112th Avenue
Miami, FL 33172
(305) 593-2778

Importers of Scotch bonnets from the Caribbean.

Quetzál Foods International
   Corp.
P.O. Box 13643
New Orleans, LA 70185
(504) 486-0830

Grower and shipper of Rica Red habaneros and mash; manufacturer of Rica Red brand products.

Seed Savers Exchange
Route 3, Box 239
Decorah, Iowa 52101

Seed Savers Exchange is dedicated to the preservation of heirloom seed varieties, including many capsicums; publisher of annual yearbook listing available varieties.

Shepherd Garden Seeds
6116 Highway 9
Felton, CA 95018
(408) 335-6910

Habanero seeds.

Stonewall Chili Pepper Co.
P.O. Box 241, Highway 290
   East
Stonewall, TX 78671-9998
(800) 232-2995

Fresh habaneros in season; dried and pickled habaneros; manufacturer of habanero sauces and products.

USDA-ARS Plant
   Introduction Station
1109 Experiment Street
Griffin, GA 30223-1797

Public may request seed of certain *chinense* varieties; include SASE with request.

Habanero Products

NOTE: A couple of these companies also sell seeds and pods.

Anjo's Imports
P.O Box 4031
Cerritos, CA 90703
(310) 865-9544

Complete line of Caribbean habanero sauces.

The Blazing Chile Brothers
3320 Trout Gulch Road
Aptos, CA 95003
(800) 473-9040

Mail-order source for habanero hot sauces.

Caribbean Food Products
1936 North Second Avenue
Jacksonville Beach, FL 32250
(904) 246-0149

Mail-order source for Trinidadian Congo pepper sauces.

Chile Pepper Magazine
P.O. Box 80780
Albuquerque, NM 87198
(800) 359-1483

Hot and spicy cookbooks available; also, subscriptions.

Coyote Cocina
1364 Rufina Circle, No. 1
Santa Fe, NM 87501
(800) 866-HOWL

Mail-order source for habanero hot sauces and other products.

Flamingo Flats
P.O. Box 441
St. Michael's, MD 21663
(800) 468-8841

Mail-order source for habanero hot sauces and jerk products.

Le Saucier
Faneuil Hall Marketplace
Boston, MA 02109
(617) 227-9649

Habanero sauces and condiments from all over the world.

Calido Chile Traders
3150 Mercier, Ste. 516
Kansas City, MO 64111
(800) 568-8468

Mail-order sources for habanero hot sauces and other products.

Old Southwest Trading Co.
P.O. Box 7545
Albuquerque, NM 87194
(505) 836-0168

Mail-order source for dried habaneros, habanero seeds, and habanero sauces and products.

Sante Fe School of Cooking
116 W. San Francisco Street
Santa Fe, NM 87501
(505) 983-4511

Mail-order source for habanero seeds, dried and pickled pods, and habanero products.

BIBLIOGRAPHY

Andrews, Jean. "Around the World with the Chili Pepper: Post Columbian Distribution of Domesticated Capsicums." *Journal of Gastronomy*, Vol. 4, No. 3 (Autumn), 21, 1988.

———. *Peppers: The Domesticated Capsicums*. Austin, TX: University of Texas Press, 1984.

Barnes, Peggy. "Caribbean Kitchens." *Chile Pepper*, 18, Jan./Feb. 1983.

Beckett-Young, Kathleen. "Jamaica Jerk: Barbecue Comes Hot, Hotter, Hottest. *San Antonio Express-News*, Feb. 18, 1990.

Benghiat, Norma. *Traditional Jamaican Cookery*. London: Penguin, 1985.

Cheng, S.S. "The Use of *Capsicum chinense* as Sweet Pepper Cultivars and Sources for Gene Transfer." In *Tomato and Pepper Production in the Tropics*, ed. by S.K. Green. Taipei: Asian Vegetable Research and Development Center, 1989.

DeGaray, Rodolfo, and Thomas Brown. "Cuban Foods that Bite Back." *Chile Pepper*, 29, Jan./Feb. 1992.

Del Castillo, Jean. "The World's Hottest Chili." *San Antonio-Express-News*, Apr. 1, 1992.

DeWitt, Dave. "Down de Islands." *Chile Pepper,* 18, Jan./Feb, 1993.

DeWitt, Dave, and Paul Bosland. *The Pepper Garden*. Berkeley, CA: Ten Speed Press, 1993.

DeWitt, Dave and Nancy Gerlach. "Expedition to Belize." *Chile Pepper*, 38, Summer, 1989.

———. "Quest for Fire: In Search of Hot Stuff in Costa Rica." *Chile Pepper*, 28, July/Aug. 1993.

———. *The Whole Chile Pepper Book*. Boston: Little, Brown, 1990.

DeWitt, Dave, and Mary Jane Wilan. *Callaloo, Calypso, and Carnival: The Cuisines of Trinidad and Tobago*. Freedom, CA: The Crossing Press, 1993.

Gonzales, Michael. "Jerk Pork Jamaica Style." *Caribbean Week*, 13, June 13–26, 1992.

Hazen-Hammond, Susan, and Eduardo Fuss. *Chile Pepper Fever: Mine's Hotter Than Yours*. Stillwater, MN: Voyageur Press, 1993.

Hilton, Anne. "Matouks Taking Trinidad Tastes to Market." *Caribbean Week,* 17, June 13-26, 1992.

Jackson-Opuku, Sandra, and Michael O. West. "Love Potions." *Carribean Travel and Life,* 38, Jan./Feb. 1994.

Karoff, Barbara. *South American Cooking.* Berkeley, CA: Aris Books, 1989.

Kopytoff, Barbara Klamon. "Maroon Jerk Pork and Other Jamaican Cooking." In *The Anthropologist's Cookbook,* ed. by Jessica Kuper. New York: Universe Books, 1977.

Laborde, Cancino, and P. Pozo Compodonico. *Presente and Pasado del Chile en Mexico.* Publicacion Especial Numero 85. Mexico City: Nac. de Invest. Agr., 1982.

Lomeli, Arturo. *El Chile y Otros Picantes.* Mexico, D. F.: Editorial Prometeo Libre, 1987.

Lucas, Eric. "Home Grown." *Alaska Airlines Magazine,* Nov. 1993.

Mars, W. B., and Carlos. Rizzini *Useful Plants of Brazil.* San Francisco: Holden-Day, 1966.

Morthland, John. "Fire Power." *Texas Monthly,* 50, Sept. 1991.

Naigai, H. "Tomato and Pepper Production in Brazil." In *Tomato and Pepper Production in the Tropics,* ed. by T. D. Griggs and B. T. McLean. Taipei: Asian Vegetable Research and Development Center, 1989.

Naj, Amal. *Peppers: A Story of Hot Pursuits.* New York: Knopf, 1992.

National Pepper Conference Newsletter. San Miguel de Allende, Mexico. Jan. 1984.

Pickersgill, Barbara. "The Archaeological Record of Chili Peppers (*Capsicum* spp.) and the Sequence of Plant Domestication in Peru." *American Antiquity,* Vol. 34, No. 1 54-61, 1969.

————. "The Domestication of Chili Peppers." In *The Domestication and Exploitation of Plants and Animals,* ed. by P. J. Ucko and G. W. Dimbleby. London: Gerald Duckworth, 1969.

————. "Migration of Chili Peppers, *Capsicum* spp., in the Americas." In *Pre-Columbian Plant Migration,* ed. by Doris Stone. Cambridge, MA: Peabody Museum of Archeology and Ethnology, Harvard University, 1984.

Purseglove, J. W., et al. "Chillies: *Capsicum* spp." In *Spices.* London: Longman's, 1981.

Raichlen. Steven. "Hot, Hot,. Hot! Caribbean Pepper Has Fire-Power." *Medina County Gazette,* June 30, 1990.

———— Miami Spice. New York: Workman Publishing, 1993.

Roach, Joe. Datil Do It." *Chile Pepper,* 14, May/June 1991.

Schindeler, Janice. "Pure Heat." *The Houston Post*, July 22, 1992.

Seed Savers Exchange. *Seed Savers Yearbook*. Decorah, IA: Seed Savers Exchange, 1983 and 1994.

Silliker Laboratories. "Laboratory Report, Red Savina Habanero 1994 Special." Sept. 3, 1994.

Smith, Paul G. and Charles B. Heiser. "Taxonomy of *Capsicum sinense* Jacq. and the Geographic Distribution of Cultivated *Capsicum* species." Bulletin of the Torrey Botanical Club, Vol. 84, No. 6, 413. Dec. 1957.

Solomon, Jay. "Pepper Power." *Caribbean Travel and Life,* 108, Mar./Apr. 1993.

———. "In Search of the Scotch Bonnet." *Chile Pepper*, 30, Jan./Feb. 1993.

Szilagyi, Pete. "Hot! On the Trail." *Austin American-Statesman*, Sept. 14, 1991.

Wine & Food Companion editors. "Hot Sauce Fever: Making Sense of the New Bottled Heat." *Wine & Food Companion*, Summer 1992.

INDEX

More *Hot Stuff* from
Ten Speed Press / Celestial Arts

THE FIERY CUISINES
by Dave DeWitt and Nancy Gerlach

"DeWitt and Gerlach seem to know everything about 'firepower' and present fine international samplings of hot and spicy dishes."
—*Booklist*

The authors' comprehensive guide to the world's most delicious hot dishes. Includes nearly 200 recipes for appetizers, condiments, soups, salads, breads, and main dishes and the history of hot spices.

$11.95 paper, 229 pages.

THE PEPPER GARDEN
by Dave DeWitt and Paul W. Bosland

The complete guide to growing your own chile peppers, whether you live in pepper-growing country or other regions. De Witt and Bosland (one of the foremost chile pepper breeders and associate professor of horticulture at New Mexico State) offer everything you need to know to grow and enjoy peppers, including variety selection tips, planting and cultivation information, and harvesting directions.

$14.95 paper, 240 pages with color photos and illustrations.

HOT PEPPERS
by Richard Schweid

"HOT PEPPERS blends facts, humor, history; its casual but informative narrative style is so enjoyable, one wonders how such a (seemingly) small subject could possibly turn out to be so interesting."
—*Seattle Post-Intelligencer*

$7.95 paper, 272 pages.

THE GREAT CHILE BOOK
by Mark Miller with John Harrisson

A full-color photographic guide to one hundred varieties of chiles— fifty each of fresh and dried, including a brief description, tips for use, and a heat rating. The book also gives a history of the chile in Mexican and Southwestern tradition, and recipes from the Coyote Cafe.

$14.95 paper, 128 pages.

CHILE PEPPER POSTERS

Created by Mark Miller of the Coyote Cafe, these sumptuous chile identification posters show thirty-one fresh chiles and thirty-five dried ones, with heat ratings and cooking tips for each. With their unique pre-Colombia borders and vivid photography, these framing-quality prints make a fabulous addition to any wall.

**Fresco (fresh) $15.00, Seco (dried) $15.00.
Set of both posters $25.00.**